"This workbook is a user-friendly self-help guide to improving sleep for trauma survivors who have developed sleep problems. I particularly like the fact that the book uses principles for sleep improvement that are empirically based, and presents them in a stepwise fashion that users will find easy to follow. While the primary audience of this book is trauma survivors themselves, I believe that trauma therapists will also find it valuable as a resource they can use directly or recommend to their clients."

—David W. Foy, Ph.D., professor of psychology at Pepperdine University in Santa Clara, CA

"Enhanced with clear worksheets and easy-to-understand, step-by-step instructions, Thompson and Franklin provide a procedurally adept, evidence-based, authoritative self-help guide to mastering complex insomnia and nightmares associated with PTSD."

—Kenneth L. Lichstein, Ph.D., professor at the University of Alabama and director of the Sleep Research Project

"This workbook provides a useful framework to guide therapists and self-help efforts. A number of useful tools for assessment and monitoring are included. The step-by-step program comprehensively addresses the thoughts and behaviors that tend to perpetuate sleep problems that are associated with PTSD."

—Thomas A Mellman, MD, professor of psychiatry at Howard University in Washington, DC, and program director of its General Clinical Research Center

"This workbook is a masterpiece and is something that mental health providers and patients have needed for a long time. It clearly provides a practical and systematic approach to addressing troublesome symptoms associated with PTSD. Mental clinics are swamped with combat veterans who need more than a pharmaceutical sleep aid."

—Dennis L. Reeves, Ph.D., retired commander in the United States Navy and clinical neuropsychologist

D1605123

"The authors have done a masterful job of addressing the various types of sleeping problems that can wreak havoc in the lives of trauma survivors. This extremely well-organized and clearly written book breaks down the complex problem of getting a good night's sleep into simple but meaningful steps. It provides an abundance of solid suggestions and alternative ways that survivors can help themselves. This superb guide to overcoming sleeping problems is chock full of information and contains many excellent worksheets and innovative approaches to the make-or-break issue of adequate sleep. I highly recommend it for clients and mental health professionals alike."

—Aphrodite Matsakis, Ph.D., post-traumatic stress disorder specialist and author of *I Can't Get Over It*

"To sleep, perchance to dream—without nightmares, racing thoughts, or interruptions. This book uses a variety of exercises to increase the likelihood of sleep while challenging habits that interfere with restful, stressless sleep. The author also provides ways to lessen repetition of trauma-related nightmares so that dreaming can again become a time of restoration, not rumination. This book will be a source of gratitude for many trauma survivors as they relearn how to sleep and, perchance, to dream!"

—Mary Beth Williams, Ph.D., LCSW, CTS, author of *The PTSD Workbook*

The
Post-Traumatic
Insomnia
Workbook

A Step-by-Step Program

for Overcoming Sleep

Problems After Trauma

KARIN ELORRIAGA THOMPSON, PH.D.
C. LAUREL FRANKLIN, PH.D.

New Harbinger Publications, Inc.

Common factors that impact sleep adapted from Morin, Charles M., and Colin A. Espie. 2003. *Insomnia: A Clinical Guide to Assessment and Treatment.* New York: KluwerAcademic/Plenum Publishers with kind permission from Springer Science and Business Media.

Calm Breathing exercise reproduced with permission of Guilford Publications, Inc., from *Treating the Trauma of Rape*, Edna B. Foa and Barbara O. Rothbaum, 1998; permission conveyed through Copyright Clearance Center Inc.

Progressive Muscle Relaxation exercise, Short Basic Progressive Muscle Relaxation exercise, Self-Hypnosis script, and Autogenic Relaxation exercise adapted with permission by New Harbinger Publications, Inc. *The Relaxation and Stress Reduction Workbook*, Martha Davis, Elizabeth Robbins Eshelman, and Matthew McKay. www.newharbinger.com.

Putting the Day to Rest technique and Bedtime Wind-Down technique adapted from Morin, Charles M., and Colin A. Espie. 2003. *Insomnia: A Clinical Guide to Assessment and Treatment.* New York: KluwerAcademic/Plenum Publishers with kind permission from Springer Science and Business Media.

Writing in Your Journal exercise adapted with permission by New Harbinger Publications, Inc. *Writing to Heal*, James W. Pennebaker. www.newharbinger.com.

Observe Your Thoughts and Experiences and Label Them exercise adapted with permission by New Harbinger Publications, Inc. *Get Out Of Your Mind and Into Your Life*, Steven C. Hayes and Spencer Smith. www.newharbinger.com.

Distributed in Canada by Raincoast Books

FSC
Mixed Sources
Product group from well-managed
forests and other controlled sources
Cert no. SW-COC-002283
www.fsc.org
© 1996 Forest Stewardship Council

Acquired by Melissa Kirk; cover design by Amy Shoup; edited by Kayla Sussel; text design by Tracy Marie Carlson

Library of Congress Cataloging-in-Publication Data

Thompson, Karin E.
    The post-traumatic insomnia workbook : a step-by-step program for overcoming sleep problems after trauma / Karin E. Thompson and C. Laurel Franklin.
        p. cm.
    Includes bibliographical references.
    ISBN 978-1-57224-893-9
    1. Insomnia--Treatment--Popular works. 2. Psychic trauma--Popular works. 3. Post-traumatic stress disorder--Popular works. I. Franklin, C. Laurel. II. Title.
    RC548.T52 2010
    616.8'49820078--dc22

                    2010020162

12 11 10   10 9 8 7 6 5 4 3 2 1   First printing

With gratitude to our families, Jeff, Hillary, Chase, and Dan. Your love and encouragement support us in all our endeavors.

Contents

Acknowledgments

We would like to acknowledge the contribution of Jeffrey West, Ph.D., who lent his expertise on chronic pain and its treatment to this book. A graduate of the University of North Carolina at Greensboro in Clinical Psychology, Dr. West developed the Chronic Pain Coping Program and is the primary supervisor for behavioral pain management training at the VA Medical Center, Memphis. He has published in areas of both clinical and experimental pain response and treatment.

In addition, we would like to acknowledge the work of the researchers and clinicians in the areas of behavioral sleep medicine and trauma, on which our work is based. We want to especially thank Dr. Kenneth Lichstein for sharing his expertise in behavioral sleep medicine and for consulting on our earlier work.

Finally, we would like to acknowledge the strength and courage of our patients, for whom this book is written.

Introduction

Congratulations on your decision to sleep better! After surviving a psychological trauma, many people experience a disruption in their ability to sleep—both in the number of hours they sleep and in their ability to feel rested following sleep. If you are among these, *The Post-Traumatic Insomnia Workbook* is a comprehensive treatment protocol based on proven techniques that will help you regain control over your sleep. If you have been struggling with sleep since surviving a traumatic event, you can look forward to sleeping better in just a few weeks by using the skills you will find in this workbook.

HOW TO USE THIS WORKBOOK

You can be sleeping better soon. This book will help educate you about the effect that traumatic experiences have on sleep. It also will provide you with step-by-step exercises and worksheets to help you identify, understand, and change your sleep problems.

The Purpose

Insomnia can be defined either as difficulty falling or staying asleep, or as poor sleep quality that occurs at least three times a week and impacts daytime functioning or causes distress (World Health Organization 1992). Individuals with trauma-related insomnia have sleep problems that begin following a traumatic or life-threatening event and that do not diminish within several months after that event. So if you didn't have problems falling or staying asleep before you survived your trauma, but you've had sleep issues since then, this workbook is for you.

Insomnia following trauma is a common symptom, and often it is not addressed by physicians or even mental health clinicians. But what starts as a short-term, normal reaction to trauma can spiral into a longer-term, chronic problem. This means that even though your traumatic experience is long past, and your life is back to normal in most ways, sleep problems can persist for a long time after the trauma. These problems lead to becoming frustrated about sleep and having to deal with the effects of sleep disruption in your life.

The good news is that insomnia following a trauma can be overcome. The premise of this book is that you can learn ways to manage and enhance both your sleep quality and quantity. The book is for individuals wanting to understand and overcome their trauma-related insomnia and for practitioners seeking more information about trauma-related insomnia to help their clients sleep better. Trauma-related sleep problems are treatable.

What This Treatment Does and Does Not Do

The Post-Traumatic Insomnia Workbook treatment works for trauma-related insomnia only. There are other sleep disorders that co-occur or can be mistaken for insomnia that will not respond to these techniques. What insomnia is and is not is described in detail in chapter 1. We recommend consulting a medical professional to determine the exact nature of your sleep problems. A sleep study using polysomnography can help to identify the sleep condition you are struggling with and can yield relevant treatment recommendations.

Understanding alone will not change your sleep pattern, but it will help you to determine which treatment is best for you. It will also help you to better implement the techniques presented in this workbook and to stay motivated to change over the course of using these techniques.

How This Book Is Organized

The chapters are intended to be read sequentially so you can begin to make changes gradually, as you finish each chapter. Most chapters can be read and implemented within one week. However, some chapters have more material in them than others, and you may want to break up the larger chapters using the worksheets and implementing your skills over a longer time period (for example, in chapter 5). Progress at your own pace. It is more important to be thorough than to be fast.

The treatment checklist in the appendix outlines all the techniques so you can be sure that you've incorporated them into your life. Photocopy this checklist and place it on your refrigerator or home office bulletin board or beside your bed to help you remember to practice the techniques you've learned.

There are two types of worksheets in this workbook. Some will help you gain a better understanding of your problems and others will help you make changes to the thoughts and behaviors that negatively impact your sleep. It is important that you use both types of worksheets.

For Clinicians

The chapters are set up sequentially so that chapters 2 through 9 represent eight distinct segments that can be completed with clients in a fifty- to sixty-minute therapy session. Some clients may need more than a week to incorporate the skills they learn in a specific chapter. It's possible to divide longer chapters into more than one therapy session (for example, chapter 7). The treatment can be administered individually or in group therapy format.

Chapter 1 has more general information for the practitioner and can also be used for client reading assignments between therapy sessions. We recommend you make each session as useful and hands-on as possible by practicing breathing and relaxation techniques during the session, as well as discussing and problem solving the obstacles with your client.

Chapter 9, written by Jeffrey West, Ph.D., addresses sleep difficulties related to chronic pain and may not apply to everyone. Also, if you notice difficulties in client compliance, you may find the strategies in chapter 10 helpful with those issues.

Using a Cognitive Behavioral Approach to Treating Your Insomnia

Cognitive behavioral therapy (CBT) is an evidence-based therapeutic approach based on the interactions among thoughts, beliefs, emotions, and behaviors and how they can influence one another. Research indicates that the CBT methods presented here are effective in treating insomnia (Morin, Bastien, and Savard 2003), including insomnia linked to medical and psychiatric problems (Lamarche and De Koninck 2007; Perlman et al. 2008). CBT for insomnia helps to change cognitions or beliefs about sleep as well as behaviors and emotions that interfere with sleep.

The two main reasons that insomnia persists following a trauma are unhelpful behaviors and unhelpful thoughts. Cognitions, or thoughts and beliefs about sleep, can both cause and worsen sleep problems. When people have sleep problems for a long time, they may develop unhelpful beliefs and thought patterns related to their sleep. For example, you may believe that you will never get a good night's sleep or that you should be able to get eight or more hours of sleep.

Similarly, you may have developed some behaviors that, although intended to help you sleep, end up getting in the way of sleep. Such behaviors might include staying in bed longer the morning after a sleepless night, napping during the day, or drinking a nightcap before going to bed to make yourself feel sleepy. The methods outlined in this book will help you to change your habits to reclaim a good night's rest.

Goals of Trauma-Related Insomnia Treatment

It is important for you to set realistic sleep goals for yourself. Most people do not get eight hours of sleep per night, every night. Setting a goal for eight hours of sleep every night is unrealistic and may cause you to become frustrated with yourself and the techniques in this workbook.

We want you to gain a better understanding of your sleep pattern and the amount of rest you require to feel your best, which may be more or less than the average person needs. Once you know your sleep pattern, you can work toward changing it to improve your sleep quality, which will lead to an enhanced sense of good health and being well rested. As you go through this workbook, we will help you to increase your awareness of your sleep habits and patterns, and to set realistic, attainable goals.

The techniques in the workbook are designed to offer opportunities for improving sleep quantity and sleep quality. The number of hours you sleep a night is your quantity of sleep. Your sleep quality reflects whether the sleep you get is restorative and leads to feeling rested and refreshed the next day. The CBT skills taught here will improve both the quality and quantity of your sleep because they're both essential to a good night's rest.

After reading this workbook, you will have:

◆ Better awareness of your sleep pattern

◆ Increased understanding of insomnia as part of trauma-related hyperarousal

◆ A full knowledge of sleep hygiene and other CBT strategies to improve sleep quality and quantity

◆ A way to cope with trauma-related nightmares

◆ A way to cope with chronic pain

EFFORT PLUS TIME EQUALS CHANGE

Understanding trauma-related insomnia will be helpful, but understanding alone will not give you a better night's rest. You must practice the techniques outlined in this workbook for your sleep patterns to change. Practice these techniques repeatedly over time, even if at first you see no change. Repetition and persistence, along with using as many of the techniques as possible, are the key to success.

It's likely that you've been hoping your sleep problems would go away without intervention, but they haven't. It's unlikely that your chronic, trauma-related sleep problems will get better without intervention if these problems have gone on for more than three months. You've probably tried out different strategies to sleep better. Effort alone does not result in better sleep. That is, sporadically applying new techniques, choosing to use some techniques but not others, and using them for only a few days and then discarding them will not result in significant changes to your sleep patterns.

The techniques in this book work best when used in combination. Incorporating all of the techniques in this workbook and repeatedly using them over time will give you the best chance to overcome insomnia by developing and practicing new sleep habits.

Sleep Logs

Using a sleep log to monitor your sleep as it progressively gets better is helpful. We have provided a sleep log entitled the Nightly Sleep Tracking Form in chapter 2. We suggest that you make several copies of this sleep log and use it to track your sleep throughout the time that you use this workbook. You may also want to make more copies and use the log for a longer period of time. Chart your sleep pattern for one week before you begin implementing the techniques. For the length of time you use this workbook, continue to chart your sleep patterns so you can see the progress you make. This will help you to stay motivated.

For practitioners, we suggest having your clients use the sleep logs to track their sleep at baseline and then for the duration of the therapy. Using the sleep log is useful for raising awareness of one's sleep pattern as well as for tracking progress and change.

Utilizing Support

If you are married or are in a committed relationship, your partner can be a valuable source of information about your insomnia and provide support for you while you work to overcome it. And as you work to change your sleep habits, your bed partner may be affected by these changes too.

In the short run, some of the changes may disturb your bed partner. However, in the long run, having a partner who sleeps well will be worth the disturbance. Having your partner support your efforts to sleep better, educating him or her about the changes you are making, and having your partner understand why these changes are important will improve your chances for success.

Of course, you may not have a partner who is disturbed by your insomnia. Nevertheless, you should read the Utilizing Support sections because there may be other people in your life who can provide important types of support to you in some of the ways we suggest.

Overcoming Obstacles and Planning for Success

Sections entitled Overcoming Obstacles and Planning for Success are designed to help you think about the obstacles you may encounter while working to overcome trauma-related insomnia. After trying a technique, thinking about the issues raised in these sections will help you solve most difficulties you may encounter.

Using the Suggested Goal Assignments

Suggested Goal Assignments are included in chapters 2 through 8. The Suggested Goal Assignments are designed to help you practice the techniques learned in each chapter without becoming overwhelmed, building a foundation for better sleep as you go. Each chapter builds on the previous chapter, so you'll master some techniques before you learn others.

The appendix has a checklist of the techniques from the entire workbook. Use this checklist as a guide to ensure that you continue using each strategy for the best sleep possible.

For practitioners using this workbook as a weekly session guide, the Goal Assignments include ways for your clients to practice what they learn between sessions. It's essential for clients to understand that the real therapy for overcoming sleep problems happens in their homes, not in the therapy sessions. Practicing these techniques is the only way to benefit from them.

It's Time to Get Started

The techniques used here employ proven strategies to improve sleep disrupted by trauma. You can overcome your sleep problems. Remember, it just takes practice and persistence. You can do it. Let's get started.

Chapter 1

Trauma-Related Sleep Problems

Developing insomnia following a traumatic, extremely stressful life experience is very common. Fortunately, overcoming insomnia following a trauma is possible. Understanding why you've developed sleep problems and the reasons your sleep problems persist are important first steps to identifying and treating your insomnia. Accordingly, in this chapter you'll learn:

- The definition of insomnia

- To define a traumatic event

- Reasons why insomnia develops after a traumatic event

- Common difficulties adjusting after a trauma

- Ways to identify sleep problems

- How trauma-related sleep problems can be overcome

INSOMNIA

The American Academy of Sleep Medicine's educational website (www.sleepeducation.com) lists four basic kinds of insomnia and related symptoms (American Academy of Sleep Medicine 2009). They are as follows.

Difficulty falling asleep. People without sleep problems take about fifteen to twenty minutes to fall asleep. If you regularly take longer than this to fall asleep, we would say that you have difficulty falling asleep.

Difficulty staying asleep. This simply means waking up frequently during the night and having problems getting back to sleep. The number of awakenings during one night varies from person to person. If you find that you awaken in the middle of the night, that you have problems returning to sleep, and that these awakenings cause you to experience daytime fatigue, it's likely that you have problems staying asleep.

Waking up too early. Problems awakening too early in the morning, coupled with an inability to fall back asleep, define this third type of insomnia.

Poor quality sleep. If you wake up and feel tired and unrefreshed, you may be getting sleep that is of poor quality. Sleep that is fragmented or broken can lead to feelings of fatigue the next day.

Other Important Insomnia Symptoms

Problems with falling or staying asleep, awakening too early, and poor sleep quality are types of insomnia. Insomnia also involves the effect that your disrupted sleep has on your daytime functioning. For example, you may be concerned that your poor sleep is causing you to experience:

- Feeling irritable or tired during the day
- Difficulty concentrating at work or school
- Daytime sleepiness
- Worry or distress about sleep problems

THE THREE-FACTOR MODEL OF INSOMNIA

Arthur Spielman and colleagues (1987) proposed three factors that contribute to insomnia: predisposing factors, precipitating factors, and perpetuating factors. Predisposing and precipitating factors explain why insomnia starts in the first place, and perpetuating factors help us to understand why insomnia can last a long time, even after the other factors have been addressed or are no longer directly influencing sleep.

Predisposing factors. These include traits or family history that might predispose one to develop insomnia. For example, if your parent or another family member had insomnia, you may have this predisposition. Or if you tend to be high-strung or a worrier, these characteristics may predispose you to insomnia. However, having predisposing factors doesn't necessarily mean you will develop insomnia in the absence of additional precipitating factors.

Precipitating factors. These include disruptive events or occurrences that may interact with predisposing factors to cause acute sleep problems. Going through a traumatic or very stressful experience is considered a precipitating factor. Most people experience some sleep disruption as a result of a precipitating factor, but typically their sleep returns to normal.

Perpetuating factors. These are mostly behavioral and involve the strategies people use in trying to stop their insomnia. Examples include using excess amounts of caffeine to remain alert during the day, drinking alcohol to relax and fall asleep, being watchful or on guard in your bedroom and staying in bed longer to try to get more sleep. Perpetuating factors account for the insomnia continuing longer than expected. Many tools and strategies address perpetuating factors in this book.

THE IMPACT OF INSOMNIA

The longer that sleep problems continue following a traumatic experience, the less likely it is that they will go away on their own. Chronic insomnia may lead to poor attention and concentration, low energy, fatigue, depression, and worry. It disrupts your life and the lives of your loved ones. It causes problems in relationships, at work or school, and in your ability to enjoy various activities.

Although understanding normal and disordered sleep is important for assessing your sleep problems and using the techniques in this workbook, understanding will not, by itself, alleviate insomnia. However, insomnia can be successfully treated.

This workbook is based on cognitive behavioral treatments for insomnia. Using similar treatments with trauma survivors resulted in improved sleep for them (Krakow, Hollifield, et al. 2001; Krakow et al. 2002). This workbook will help you to understand your specific trauma-related sleep problems. You'll learn strategies to change your sleep by making changes to your post-trauma sleep habits and to the thoughts and behaviors that contribute to or maintain your sleep problems.

THE EXPERIENCE OF PSYCHOLOGICAL TRAUMA

Traumatic life experiences are not uncommon in today's society. On a daily basis, we can watch TV news or read articles on the Internet and learn about traumatic, emotionally distressing events that are happening all over the world. According to the National Comorbidity Survey, a large study of adults in the United States, 61 percent of men and 51 percent of women reported at least one traumatic event at some point in their lifetime (Kessler et al. 1995). So psychological trauma is a more common occurrence than you may have previously thought it to be.

Traumatic experiences can be a one-time occurrence (such as a motor vehicle accident) or multi-incident (such as combat in the military or physical abuse or neglect). These are the most common traumas that people experience:

- Witnessing someone being badly injured or killed

- Being involved in a fire, flood, or natural disaster

- Being involved in a life-threatening accident

- Engaging in wartime combat

Sexual or physical assault and childhood or adult physical abuse or neglect are less common, but they can be even more pernicious and damaging than the more common traumas.

How People Are Affected by Trauma

Any traumatic experience can lead to short-term or longer-term adjustment difficulties, which is not surprising since going through a traumatic experience can cause physiological, emotional, and behavioral changes. Although most people find that they feel more like themselves within a few months after a trauma, some trauma survivors will develop post-traumatic stress disorder (PTSD) symptoms. The percentage of people who develop PTSD after a trauma varies and depends on many factors, including the nature of the trauma, but it ranges from about 10 to 40 percent (Norris and Slone 2007).

PTSD symptoms are anxiety problems that interfere with a person's ability to function. PTSD is characterized by several symptom clusters including re-experiencing the trauma in distressing ways (nightmares, flashbacks, intrusive thoughts); avoidance of reminders and emotional numbing; and significant physiological overarousal, including sleep disturbance (*American Psychiatric Association* 2000).

Although PTSD often involves sleep problems, not everyone with sleep problems after a trauma has PTSD. It may be important for you to self-assess your symptoms of PTSD and other problems that may follow a traumatic event. These problems are not addressed in this workbook; but if you have several issues that are interfering with your ability to move forward, it's important to discuss them with your medical or mental health provider. If you have some of the problems listed below, this workbook can help you to overcome insomnia; but problems other than insomnia are unlikely to change simply by working with the techniques in this book and you may need to see a professional.

SYMPTOMS OF PTSD

Symptoms of PTSD can interfere with a person's ability to function at work, with friends and family, and in other important ways. Use the checklist below to determine whether you have any of the symptoms of PTSD.

PTSD Symptoms

_____ Upsetting thoughts or intrusive memories about the traumatic event

_____ Distressing dreams about the traumatic event

_____ Feeling as if the traumatic experience were happening again

_____ Becoming emotionally upset by reminders of the trauma

_____ Feeling tension or stress in your body when reminded of the trauma

_____ Avoiding thoughts, emotions, and conversations about the trauma

_____ Avoiding people, places, and activities that arouse recollections of the trauma

_____ Inability to recall important aspects of the trauma

_____ Diminished interest in previously enjoyed activities

_____ Emotional numbing

_____ Feeling distant from others

_____ A sense that your future will be cut short or that you have no future

_____ Extreme irritability or anger

_____ Diminished ability to concentrate

_____ Being overly watchful or on guard

_____ Exaggerated startle response

_____ Difficulty sleeping

SYMPTOMS OF DEPRESSION AND SUBSTANCE ABUSE

Other consequences of trauma can be related to feeling sad or depressed, substance abuse (including alcohol, legal, illegal, or prescribed drugs), or other mental health disturbances. Use the two checklists below to determine whether depression or substance abuse apply to you.

Depression Symptoms

_____ Feelings of sadness

_____ Feeling hopeless

_____ Feelings of guilt or worthlessness

_____ Appetite or weight change

_____ Loss of interest in life

_____ Feeling slowed down

_____ Feeling agitated or restless

_____ Sleeping too much or not enough

_____ Having problems concentrating

_____ Feeling a loss of energy

_____ Thoughts of death or suicide*

* If you have thoughts of suicide, call your mental health professional or report to the nearest emergency room. Or call 911 or the National Suicide Prevention Lifeline at 800-273-8255.

Substance Abuse Symptoms

_____ Drinking or using substances in situations that may be dangerous (for example, while driving or providing child care)

_____ Important people in your life objecting to your drinking or substance use

_____ Legal problems such as citations for driving under the influence (DUIs), or arrests due to drinking or substance use

_____ Using legal or prescribed drugs in excess or as an escape

_____ Unsuccessful attempts to cut down or stop drinking or drug use

_____ Blackouts or substance use causing or worsening mood problems

_____ Tolerance to the effects of alcohol or other substances (needing to use more to get the same high)

Many people who survive a trauma recover naturally over time. You may have some of the symptoms noted above as part of the normal recovery process. Short-term distress and adjustment are normal aspects of healing from trauma. However, significant mental health problems that last more than a few months and cause problems in your work or home life might require the help of a professional.

HOW CAN YOU FIND A MENTAL HEALTH PROFESSIONAL IN YOUR COMMUNITY?

If you are having significant trauma-related mental health symptoms, you should seek the assistance of a mental health professional in your community. This workbook can be used to augment other mental health treatment.

You have several options for finding a mental health professional in your community. Start by asking your primary care provider for recommendations. Check with your health insurance company, as most offer a list of preferred mental health providers. Ask family members, friends, or others you trust for recommendations. See the resources section at the end of the book for recommended professional organizations.

HOW TRAUMA IMPACTS SLEEP

Although most trauma survivors do not develop full-blown PTSD or other significant emotional problems, about 70 to 75 percent of trauma survivors report problems with insomnia (Krakow et al. 2007; North et al. 1999).

Hyperarousal, Nightmares, and Changing Your Behavior

One difficulty that often develops after trauma is hyperarousal, a state of high psychological and physical tension. In this state, your body continues to react as if danger were still present, even though there is no imminent danger and you are in a relatively safe situation. People with post-trauma hyperarousal might be more easily stressed or quicker to react than others.

It makes sense that if your body is in a high state of alertness, you will have trouble relaxing and falling asleep. Being able to sleep requires being able to relax, and hyperarousal makes relaxation and sleep more difficult. Reducing hyperarousal and encouraging your body to return to a lower state of alertness helps to reduce and manage stress and to improve sleep.

Indicators of hyperarousal may include a heightened startle response, irritability, watchfulness or being on guard, concentration problems, and sleep disturbance. Some research suggests that hyperarousal after trauma predicts subsequent severity of other post-trauma psychological symptoms and that reducing hyperarousal might help people recover over the long run (Schell, Marshall, and Jaycox 2004). Specifically, post-trauma sleep problems are thought to play a role in the development of PTSD. Likewise, the treatment of post-trauma sleep disturbance has resulted in a reduction of other PTSD symptoms (Lamarche and De Koninck 2007).

After a traumatic experience, trauma survivors often see an increase in their general arousal and watchfulness. Experiencing a trauma is an emotional shock that threatens our sense of safety in the world. In our experience, *hypervigilance*, or being overly alert and watchful, is one of the post-trauma symptoms that most interferes with sleep. Chapter 3 discusses hypervigilance and how to reduce it to improve sleep.

Nightmares or scary dreams that resemble an aspect of the trauma also account for many sleep problems. Nightmares can awaken us and be frightening. Some people find that their nightmares disturb their bed partner. Nightmares may be a way that your mind processes and makes sense of your traumatic experience. Chapter 8 discusses coping with nightmares.

Often, after a short period of sleep disturbance, people try to cope with their sleep disruption by changing their behaviors. For example, after you've had a poor night's sleep, have you ever decided to take a nap the next day to catch up with the sleep you lost? Have you ever had a drink or two before bedtime to help you relax and fall asleep? Although these strategies make sense at first glance, over time these coping behaviors may add to your sleep distress.

Whether your sleep disturbance is a part of PTSD, depression, or general post-trauma adjustment difficulties, it's important to address your sleep problems as soon as possible. There is some evidence that sleep problems after trauma may lead to other problems such as PTSD, depression, and physical symptoms (Harvey and Bryant 1998; Mohr et al. 2003). Although it is impossible to predict the course of trauma recovery for anyone, if you are having significant sleep problems, it's best to deal with this as soon as possible.

The first question to ask yourself is whether you are sleeping differently than before your trauma. If the answer is yes, then you may have the sort of sleep problems that will respond to this therapy. Talk to your medical provider to be sure you have no medical conditions or medication issues that are causing your sleep problems. (See chapter 5 for a list of medications that may impact sleep.)

UNDERSTANDING NORMAL SLEEP

Understanding normal sleep will help you to put your trauma-related sleep problems into context and set realistic goals for yourself using this workbook's treatment program.

Sleep normally progresses through a series of five stages repeatedly throughout the night. Stages 1 and 2 are light sleep and stages 3 and 4 are deep sleep. REM (rapid eye movement) sleep, the fifth stage, occurs when we dream and the brain processes information. When sleep is measured physiologically, each of the stages has its particular characteristics. Some basic facts about sleep stages, based on scientific knowledge, appear below.

Stage 1. After you become drowsy, you move into this first phase of sleep. As you drift in and out of consciousness, your sleep is light and you're easily awakened. Your brain waves start slowing down. Your breathing and heart rate slow down, your blood pressure decreases, and your body temperature falls. Your eyes move slowly during this stage. Muscle activity slows down. Sometimes during stage 1, muscles contract and cause a sensation of falling. This stage lasts about five minutes.

Stage 2. Your brain waves slow down even more during stage 2, although there are occasional bursts of brain activity. During this time you have the sensation that you are falling asleep. For most people, this stage lasts ten to fifteen minutes.

Stage 3. In this stage of deep sleep, your brain waves are extremely slow (delta waves), but they're punctuated by smaller, faster waves. It is difficult to awaken people from this stage of sleep.

Stage 4. In stage 4, your brain produces only slow, delta waves. You have no eye movement or muscle activity during this stage. As in stage 3, you're in a deep sleep and it's very difficult to awaken you during stage 4. Together, stages 3 and 4 last twenty to forty minutes.

REM Sleep. This is a period of deep sleep characterized by rapid eye movements. Your muscles become paralyzed but your brain is very active. Your breathing becomes more rapid, shallow, and irregular. Your heart rate and blood pressure increase, and sexual arousal is common. Most of your dreams occur during REM sleep. Some think that REM sleep is linked to learning and memory and maybe even to the resolution of emotional conflict (Morin and Espie 2003). People with post-trauma symptoms may experience a disruption in REM sleep (Engdahl et al. 2000; Mellman et al. 2002).

Over the course of a night, you cycle through these sleep stages several times. Deep sleep (stages 3 and 4) is more prominent in the first third of the night, and REM is more prominent in the later phases of sleep.

COMMON FACTORS THAT IMPACT SLEEP

Many factors affect sleep. Here's a summary of these factors and how they impact sleep (adapted from Morin and Espie 2003, with kind permission from Springer Science and Business Media).

Aging

Normal aging produces changes in sleep patterns. Older adults spend more time in stages 1 and 2 and, as a result, have more frequent awakenings. As you age, you spend less and less time in deep sleep and REM sleep. These changes become noticeable in your forties. Older adults take longer to fall asleep, spend more time in bed awake, and have fewer hours of total sleep (Morgan 2000).

Medical Conditions and Medications

Sleep problems may be a sign of (or worsened by) a variety of medical problems. The following medical conditions are known to disrupt sleep (Morin and Espie 2003): cardiovascular problems, chronic pain, endocrine disorders, neurological disorders, and pulmonary disorders. Other common sleep disorders must be considered as well. Narcolepsy, obstructive sleep apnea, periodic limb movement, and restless legs syndrome are some common sleep disorders that require medical attention. Struggling to stay awake during the day is more commonly a result of these conditions than insomnia and may indicate the need for medical intervention.

Medications can also cause sleep problems. See chapter 5 for a list of medications that may impact sleep. If you are taking any of these medications or are not sure whether you have any of these medical problems, talk to your medical provider before starting to work with the treatments in this workbook.

Psychosocial Factors

In addition to severe traumatic events that impact sleep, stressful life events can also lead to sleep disruption. Life changes, including joyful events, such as having a new baby, moving into a new home, or getting married, as well as losses or stressful events, such as losing your job, getting a divorce, losing a loved one, or having money problems can disrupt the delicate sleep cycle. Most sleep problems resolve on their own after a short time. However, for some people these problems can last longer than the stressor itself.

Lifestyle and Environmental Factors

Chapter 5 discusses behavioral and environmental factors that affect your ability to fall and stay asleep. These lifestyle factors are habits that, although inconsequential before your trauma, may now interfere with your sleep. These may include watching television in the bedroom or using alcohol to induce sleep. Environmental factors are elements in your home or bedroom that may not be conducive to sleep, such as air quality and temperature in the bedroom.

HOW MUCH SLEEP IS ENOUGH?

You might ask yourself whether you are getting enough sleep. Most of us have heard that we need eight hours of sleep to stay healthy and feel rested. While seven to eight hours of sleep per night is about average for most adults, sleep needs vary tremendously. Determine your sleep need by charting your sleep with the Nightly Sleep Tracking Form (in chapter 2) and pay attention to how rested you feel in the morning.

Also examine your degree of alertness throughout the day. If you aren't falling asleep during the day while you are at work or doing other important activities, you're probably getting enough sleep. Some people feel refreshed and rested after only four hours of sleep; others need nine or ten hours. Many people fall somewhere in between. It isn't helpful to hold yourself to an arbitrary standard or to someone else's standard. However, even if you're getting enough total hours of sleep, you may not be getting the best quality or the most refreshing sleep.

Chapter 2

Assessing Your Sleep Patterns, Setting Goals, and Getting Started

You can't change what you don't understand. Therefore, having a full understanding of your sleep problems is an important first step to overcoming them. This chapter includes a brief assessment that will help you achieve a more complete understanding of your sleep problems. Then you will use the worksheets to set realistic and attainable sleep goals for yourself. The objectives for this chapter are to:

◆ Assess your sleep difficulties

◆ Understand your sleep problems

◆ Begin working toward improved sleep

ASSESS YOUR SLEEP PATTERNS AND THE QUALITY OF YOUR SLEEP

It's likely that you spend a lot of time thinking and worrying about your sleep problems. However, it is unlikely that you completely understand them. At this stage in your planning for change, it's important for you to begin formally assessing your sleep problems. Increasing your understanding will help you use the techniques in this book as effectively as possible. The following Trauma Insomnia Quiz will help you to better understand your sleep.

To answer the questions, place a check mark in the appropriate box to the right of the question.

Trauma Insomnia Quiz		
Do you lie awake in bed for more than 30 minutes before falling asleep?	[✓] Yes	[ ] No
Do you awaken in the middle of the night for more than five to ten minutes and have difficulty falling back to sleep?	[✓] Yes	[ ] No
Do you awaken more than an hour before you want to in the morning?	[✓] Yes	[ ] No
Are you irritable or grumpy on days when you don't sleep well?	[✓] Yes	[ ] No
Do you feel overly tired during the day or when you first wake up?	[✓] Yes	[ ] No
Do you worry about your lack of sleep and its impact on your day-to-day activities?	[✓] Yes	[✓] No
Do you lie awake at night listening to noises or thinking about danger?	[ ] Yes	[✓] No
Do you get up at night to check your doors or windows?	[✓] Yes	[ ] No
Did the start of these sleep problems coincide with a traumatic experience?	[✓] Yes	[ ] No

Scoring: If you answered yes to one or more of the questions above, you have no medical conditions causing your inability to sleep, and your sleep problems began following a traumatic event, then you may have trauma-related insomnia. It's important for you to gain a better understanding of your individual pattern of trauma-related insomnia, but this may be difficult, because you cannot observe yourself sleeping. For that reason, we've included the Nightly Sleep Tracking Form here to help you assess your sleeping patterns as objectively as possible.

Tracking Your Sleep

We suggest tracking your insomnia for at least one entire week before you begin using the techniques from this workbook. The longer you track your sleep, the more likely it will provide an accurate assessment of your insomnia, so we suggest that you photocopy at least ten additional forms for your use.

Tracking your sleep for at least a week before starting the treatment will give you a good baseline assessment. This means that you'll have a good understanding of your individual pattern of trauma-related insomnia before you begin treatment. Then if you continue using the Nightly Sleep Tracking Form each week thereafter, you'll be able to judge objectively how the treatment is affecting your sleep pattern. This will help you make changes to your use of the workbook techniques and will also help keep you motivated to change.

The Nightly Sleep Tracking Form charts your sleep each night for seven consecutive nights. Although the form begins with Sunday night, you can begin on any night and then fill in the appropriate column for each day over the week. It's best to keep the Form by your bed and to try to get into the habit of completing it each day. We suggest completing the Behaviors Affecting Sleep part of the log just before bedtime as part of your bedtime routine. We also suggest completing the Sleep Quality and Quantity part of the log when you awaken in the morning. The sooner you complete this section after you wake up, the more likely you are to make an accurate assessment.

Nightly Sleep Tracking Form

Nightly Sleep Tracking Form: Week _____

Keep this tracking form beside your bed. Complete the Behaviors Affecting Sleep part of this log each night as part of your bedtime routine. Complete the Sleep Quality and Quantity part each morning after you awaken.

	Sunday	Monday	Tuesday	Wednesday	Thursday	Friday	Saturday
Behaviors Affecting Sleep							
If you napped today, how long was your nap?							
Did you take a medication that affects sleep? If so, what time of day?							
Did you use alcohol before bedtime?							
Did you use caffeine within four hours of bedtime?							
Did you exercise today? If so, what time of day did you exercise?							
Did you use nicotine just before bed or when you awakened in the night?							
Sleep Quality and Quantity							
What time did you get into bed?							

What time did you fall asleep?							
How many times in the night did you awaken?							
What was the total number of minutes you were awake in the middle of the night?							
How many dreams do you remember having during the night?							
What time did you wake up in the morning?							
What time did you get out of bed for the day?							
Did you sleep in your own bed?							
How restorative or refreshing was your sleep?*							
How many total hours did you sleep?**							

To calculate average restoration level and average sleep hours, add numbers from Sunday to Saturday and divide by 7.

Total sleep restoration level: _____ ÷ 7 = _____ average restoration level

Total hours of sleep for the week: _____ ÷ 7 = _____ average hours per night

* On a scale of 1 to 10, with 10 being the most refreshing sleep, estimate how restful or replenished you feel from last night's sleep.

** You can calculate this by counting from the time you fell asleep until you got up for the day minus the total minutes you were awake in the night.

23

Examine your Nightly Sleep Tracking Form at the end of the first week of charting your sleep. Think about any changes to your sleep patterns that you've noticed since your traumatic experience. It's likely your sleep has changed since your trauma in predictable ways that will respond to the treatments in this book.

Use the following questions to increase your understanding of your baseline sleep pattern, changes to your sleep pattern since your trauma, and those factors that currently worsen your sleep pattern. Developing insight into your sleep pattern and related factors will help you understand how your sleep has been disrupted by trauma. Such insight, in turn, will encourage you to implement the techniques in this workbook.

1. (a) How many hours of sleep did you typically get before your traumatic experience?

    _8_

   (b) Did you feel rested after a typical night's sleep before the trauma?

    _y-s_

2. (a) Currently, how many hours of sleep do you get on an average night?

    _5_

   (b) About how long are you in bed before you fall asleep?

    VARIES - 15 min -- 1Hr

   (c) Do you feel frustrated while lying in bed?

    Some

   (d) Do you watch the clock?

    Some - when I can't get to sleep

   (e) What behaviors do you engage in to try to fall asleep (for example, drinking a nightcap, watching TV in bed, going to bed earlier, staying in bed longer)?
    Tired

3. (a) Once you fall asleep, how long do you stay asleep before awakening?

    _4Hr_

(b) How many times do you awaken on a typical night?

_3-4_

(c) What do you do upon awakening in the middle of the night or in the early morning hours?

Look AT CLOCK - oFTen Same Time = peanick

4. (a) Do you have nightmares that remind you of your traumatic experience?

LESS Frequan nm-

(b) Do you wake up during or after a nightmare?

VARIES

(c) How long are you awake after a nightmare before you fall back asleep?

_?_

5. (a) Do you take naps during the day?

_No_

(b) Do you sleep in places other than your bed (for example, your sofa or recliner)?

_N_

6. Do medical conditions contribute to your sleep problems (for example, sleep apnea, sleep movement disorders, chronic pain)?

_N_

7. What have you tried to improve your sleep (for example, over-the-counter medications, prescription medications, or changing your habits or behaviors)?

FOOD chAnge - Luug= ms/l

GOAL SETTING

When you begin to make any kind of change, goal setting is essential because deciding where you want to end up helps you to get there. Setting realistic and attainable goals is equally important. As you learned in chapter 1, individual sleep needs vary from four to ten hours per night. Remember, your sleep may have changed not only because of your trauma, but also because of your normal aging since your trauma, as well as other factors (such as medical problems) which are discussed in chapter 1.

Individual differences in sleep patterns are hard to determine, but setting an unrealistically high goal for yourself may lead to frustration both with yourself and with the treatments in this workbook. However, we'll help you set concrete, realistic, and attainable goals for yourself. Use the Sleep Goals Checklist below for this purpose. Check off the goals you are willing to commit to, and put two check marks beside the goals most important to you.

Sleep Goals Checklist

_____ I will improve my environment to promote the best sleep possible for myself.

_____ I will change any bad habits that prevent me from sleeping well.

_____ I will form new habits that will improve my sleep.

_____ I will get out of bed if I don't fall asleep within about fifteen minutes.

_____ I will get enough hours of sleep each night to feel rested in the morning.

_____ If I awaken during the night, I will return to sleep quickly.

_____ I will stop sleeping in other places in my house (armchair, sofa) and limit my sleeping to my bedroom because I want to sleep when I am in my bed.

_____ I will enhance my ability to cope with nightmares.

_____ I will feel rested and refreshed most mornings.

_____ I will trust that I can function well with less than my ideal level of sleep.

_____ I will not worry or feel distressed if, on occasion, I have a poor night's sleep.

_____ Other (write any other goals you have here): _____

_____

UTILIZING SUPPORT

After completing the Trauma Insomnia Quiz and the Sleep Goals Checklist in this chapter, share this and other information you gather with your significant other. Ask your bed partner what patterns he or she has noticed while you are sleeping. Significant others often have very helpful information that you may not be aware of, because you cannot observe yourself sleeping. Talk to your partner about the following issues that may complicate your insomnia:

1. Snoring or breathing changes

2. Tossing and turning in bed

3. Acting out physically or "fighting" in your sleep

4. Talking in your sleep

5. Sleepwalking

It also can be very helpful for your partner to track your sleep using the Nightly Sleep Tracking Form. This would give you extra information to help with setting your goals.

Note: It's possible that if you're engaging in any of the behaviors listed above, your significant other's sleep is also being disrupted. It might be useful for your bed partner to track his or her own sleep and use the techniques from this workbook to sleep better. Finally, remember to discuss your findings with your medical provider so that he or she can help you determine the specific nature of your sleep problems.

It's important to discuss your goals and treatment plan with your partner. Show him or her your Sleep Goals Checklist and discuss a timeline to implement these strategies. Inform your partner that you'll continue to discuss your insomnia and sleep treatment as you continue working through this workbook and that you may ask for additional help over the course of this treatment.

If you don't have a spouse or bed partner, you can still benefit from discussing your sleep with others as you begin to use the tools in this workbook. You can ask close friends or colleagues who know you well how you behave after a poor or good night's rest. Ask for feedback on changes in your performance and mood as you begin sleeping better.

OVERCOMING OBSTACLES AND PLANNING FOR SUCCESS

At the beginning of anything new, feelings of anxiety or being overwhelmed can emerge. This is normal and doesn't last. This workbook is designed for you to overcome trauma-related insomnia slowly, at whatever pace you find comfortable.

Don't take on too much at one time, as this can lead to increased feelings of being overwhelmed. Resist the urge to try everything at once; instead, build slowly on your successes. We suggest completing one chapter a week.

Start a schedule of first reading a chapter and then using the remainder of that week to implement the skills you learned. If you haven't mastered them by the end of the week, spend another week practicing and utilizing the skills until you are comfortable with them. Once you've implemented the strategies in one chapter, move to the next.

This workbook was written to be used sequentially, moving from chapter 1 to 10. However, it isn't necessary for you to implement the skills in this suggested order. Moreover, it's possible that some sections will not directly apply to your situation (for example, chapter 9 is for individuals coping with chronic pain). What we do know is that it's important that you utilize all of your relevant skills to help you sleep better. Remember that a piecemeal approach to overcoming insomnia will not have as good results as using the skills together.

Set aside time in your daily schedule to read through the chapters in this workbook and put the strategies into practice. Some strategies require practice throughout the day, while others can be done at the same time each day. Commit now to setting aside time during the coming week to read chapter 3. Later, you can set aside time to practice the strategies you will learn.

SUGGESTED GOAL ASSIGNMENT

Practice the following assignments to improve your sleep. Remember, practicing assignments will lead to improved sleep!

1. Increase your understanding of your sleep pattern by completing the Trauma Insomnia Quiz.

2. Begin to chart your sleep using the Nightly Sleep Tracking Form.

3. Ask yourself important questions about the quality of your sleep.

4. Ask your partner, if applicable, questions about your sleep, as well as the impact it has on his or her sleep. Have your partner help you track your sleep using the Nightly Sleep Tracking Form, so you'll have more information.

5. Set realistic goals for yourself using the Sleep Goals Checklist.

6. Share your sleep goals with your partner.

Chapter 3

Your Bedroom Is for Sleep: De-Stress It!

When you have chronic sleep problems, your bedroom becomes a place of struggle and frustration, rather than a place to relax and sleep. It is important for you to reclaim your bedroom for sleep. In this chapter you will:

- ◆ Learn how trauma-related anxiety can intrude into your bedroom

- ◆ Learn a breathing technique for calming yourself

- ◆ Learn the importance of using your bedroom only for sleep

- ◆ Identify which activities are okay for the bedroom and which are better done in another room

- ◆ Identify overly vigilant behaviors that interfere with sleep

- ◆ Learn the fifteen-minute rule

HOW TO FEEL SLEEPY IN BED

Your brain is attuned to cues or signals in your environment. For example, when you smell a particular food cooking, the odor may cause you to recall a happy childhood memory. Environmental cues such as smells, sights, and sounds can elicit strong emotional reactions. Your bedroom is a powerful environmental cue. It isn't uncommon for people with insomnia to experience their bedroom as a cue for frustration and anxiety rather than a cue for rest and relaxation.

If you had no trouble sleeping before your traumatic experience, your bedroom was strongly associated with sleep. What is your bedroom associated with now? If, since the trauma, you feel drowsy and sleepy before getting into bed, but once you are in bed you feel awake and alert, your bedroom may no longer be associated with sleep. You may benefit from reestablishing cues that tell your brain your bedroom is for sleeping.

Let's take a look at why post-trauma sleep problems can be caused at least partly by bedroom cues. Consider Donna's experience.

◆ *Donna's Story*

Donna came home one evening to find that someone had broken into her house. The lock on the front door was broken and her television and stereo were gone. She was upset and called the police to report the burglary. When the police left, Donna knew she did not want to stay in her house alone that night, so she spent the night at a friend's.

The next day the door and lock were fixed, and over the next few days she installed a security system and floodlights to increase the security of her home. She also reported the burglary to the neighborhood patrol so they would spend more time watching her house. For about two weeks after the burglary, Donna had difficulty feeling safe inside her house. She didn't sleep as well as she usually did. After about two weeks, her anxiety began to subside. She felt increasingly secure in her house, especially after she learned that a suspect had been caught and was in jail. She was no longer aware of feeling anxious or fearful at home.

However, to her surprise and dismay, her sleep didn't return to normal. Instead, Donna continued struggling with falling and staying asleep. She thought more about sleep during the day, worrying about what the night would hold and how her lack of sleep was affecting her appearance and her work. She began to notice that as bedtime approached, she felt increasing dread and anxiety.

Once in bed, she found herself trying to force herself to sleep, looking at the clock every few minutes, and worrying about the problems she would have if she didn't get to sleep. Donna lay awake for hours before finally dozing off.

There are four important aspects to Donna's story:

◆ Her trauma occurred in her house. Her initial anxiety was triggered by being anywhere in her home, including her bedroom.

◆ Her anxiety about being in the house decreased over time as a result of extra security precautions and her recognition that the probability of a recurrence was low.

◆ Even after the danger was removed (burglar jailed, security increased) and she felt like her old self, Donna continued having sleep problems.

◆ She began to dread bedtime, and once in bed, she felt tense and worried.

If your traumatic experience took place in your house or especially in your bedroom, it's understandable that you may no longer feel secure in your house or bedroom. Your brain and body react with anxiety when you are there. Anxiety is a normal emotion commonly described as feeling nervous, fearful, worried, or stressed. For most people, this anxiety will decrease over time. However, sleep problems can be maintained even when there is an overall decrease in anxiety.

You may now be worried or nervous that you will not sleep at night. You might ruminate about how your lack of sleep affects you, and you may become increasingly tense as bedtime gets closer. Eventually, you dread lying down at night, and you feel tense and desperate when you're in bed. Your bed is no longer associated with calm relaxation and sleep, but rather with fear, frustration, and worry. Although the original problem that caused the insomnia has been addressed, your insomnia persists.

Anticipating frustration about sleeping makes it more likely that sleep problems will occur. When sleep disturbance persists for a period of time, a type of conditioning occurs so that you learn to associate the bedroom with fear, disappointment, and being awake, rather than with sleep. This is called *conditioned insomnia*.

When that happens, simply going to bed and preparing to sleep can lead to negative feelings and your chance for sleep decreases. Conditioned insomnia helps explain why it might be easier for you to fall asleep in front of the TV than in your own bed (Hauri and Linde 1996). For overcoming trauma-related insomnia, reconditioning your brain and changing your sleep cues is essential.

Many people had no difficulty sleeping prior to their traumatic experience. Instead, they had a firm association between their bed and peaceful sleep. Their bedroom cues were strongly associated with sleep. This association was disrupted by their traumatic experiences. If this is the case for you, this workbook can be used to recapture that association and help you to feel sleepy in bed again, instead of feeling fearful and apprehensive.

CALM BREATHING

Calm breathing is a simple tool that we'll ask you to start using now and continue using throughout your work with this book. Calm breathing can be a very useful strategy for managing stress and anxiety. You might have noticed that when you are nervous or frightened, you breathe faster. When people are frightened or stressed, they take in more oxygen to fuel the body for action. When people are relaxed, their breathing slows down.

Edna Foa and Barbara Rothbaum (2001) teach a technique called breathing retraining, which slows down breathing and focuses on the exhalation, or out-breath. You can learn to be more relaxed and feel less anxious by practicing one of the calm breathing exercises outlined below. (Reproduced with permission of Guilford Publications, Inc., from *Treating the Trauma of Rape*, Edna B. Foa and Barbara O. Rothbaum, 1998; permission conveyed through Copyright Clearance Center, Inc.)

EXERCISE: Calm Breathing 1

To breathe calmly, you'll practice three strategies while breathing in and out through your nose.

1. Focus on the out-breath by exhaling slowly until all the air is out of your lungs.

2. Slow down your breathing by pausing for a count of four after the out-breath.

3. While exhaling, say a relaxing word to yourself (for example, "calm," "relax," or "peace").

First, take a normal breath in through your nose, and then let out a long breath, also through your nose, saying your relaxing word silently to yourself while you slowly exhale all of the air in your lungs. Then, pause for a count of four before taking another in-breath.

Normal breath in. Long breath out, "reeelaaax." Pause, two, three, four.

Do this three times.

EXERCISE: Calm Breathing 2

Some people notice an increase in their ability to relax when they add an additional pause after the inhale.

1. Slow down your breathing by pausing for a count of four after the in-breath and again after the out-breath.

2. Focus on the out-breath by exhaling slowly until all the air is out of your lungs.

3. While exhaling, say a word to yourself that you find relaxing (for example, "calm," "relax," or "peace").

Normal breath in. Pause, two, three, four. Long breath out, "reeelaaax." Pause, two, three, four.

Do this three times.

EXERCISE: Calm Breathing 3

If you have breathing problems or feel uncomfortable doing the two exercises above, try taking normal breaths in and out through your nose, pausing after the exhale. You also can vary the length of your pause if a count of four is too long.

Normal breath in. Normal breath out. Pause, two, three, four.

Do this three times.

Experiment with the calm breathing exercises and see which works best for you. At first, you may want to make an audio recording of these instructions to facilitate your practice, but ultimately you will want to practice this exercise without a tape.

In addition to practicing calm breathing to facilitate sleep when you're lying in bed at night, use it during the day to help you calm down when you feel anxious or stressed. It will also help to first practice when you're already relaxed. Get into a comfortable position and focus only on your breathing. Close your eyes or focus on a spot in front of you. Practice for one to three minutes, three times a day for a total of about ten minutes daily. The more you practice, the more you'll be able to use your breathing to calm down when anxious or stressed.

In the rest of this chapter, you will learn ways to de-stress your bedroom by strengthening the association between your bedroom and sleep. Sleep researcher Richard Bootzin and his colleagues developed many of the following strategies (Bootzin and Epstein 2000).

USE YOUR BEDROOM ONLY FOR SLEEP AND SEX

To cope with being awake during the night, many individuals with chronic insomnia engage in behaviors in the bedroom that actually contribute to their insomnia. To take back your bedroom for sleep, check to see whether you are doing anything in your bedroom that interferes with your ability to sleep.

A list of wakeful activities that interfere with sleep appears below. Check off any that you do in your bedroom:

____✓____ Watch TV

_____ Argue or have difficult discussions with your significant other

_____ Read

_____ Eat

_____ Use the computer

_____ Pay bills or balance your checkbook

_____ Watch the clock

_____ Engage in overly vigilant behaviors (listening for sounds of danger, positioning the bed to face the door, keeping a weapon in your bedroom)

Sleep and sex are the only two activities that your bedroom should be used for. Avoid engaging in any alerting or wakeful activities in your bed or bedroom. Any activity that engages your brain or makes you think is considered a wakeful activity.

Using this strategy will teach your brain that your bed and bedroom are places for sleep and rest and strengthen the cues that your bedroom is for sleep instead of other activities. Here are some suggestions about how to put this strategy into practice.

Activity	Solution
Watching TV	Remove the TV from your bedroom.
Arguing	Take the argument into another room.
Reading	Set up a comfortable chair in another room.
Eating	Eat nighttime snacks in the kitchen or while doing a restful activity in another room.
Using the computer	Remove the computer from your bedroom.
Paying bills	Set up a desk or workstation in another room.
Watching the clock	Turn your clock toward the wall or put it on the floor so it is not easily seen.
Listening for sounds of danger	Use a white noise machine, fan, or other monotonous noise to eliminate extraneous sounds.
Keeping weapons in bedroom	Use the Weapon Removal Change Form, found later in this chapter.

AVOID SLEEPING ANYWHERE EXCEPT YOUR BEDROOM

You are a creature of habit. If you've been sleeping (or napping) in another room (such as on the sofa in front of your TV), then the association your brain makes between your bed and sleep is weakened. If your goal is to sleep in your bed, then you want to reteach yourself to fall asleep when you get into bed. This means making the strongest possible association for yourself between your bed and sleep.

You may have observed other ways that your brain has been trained to respond to cues. Perhaps you've noticed that when you get into a favorite chair, you instantly feel more relaxed, or when you smell a certain food cooking, the scent conjures up happy memories. That's because your brain is responding to cues in the room reminding it of what to do or how to feel.

Since your brain has lost its cue to become sleepy in the bedroom, it needs to be retrained to respond to bedroom cues. If you avoid sleeping in any other room, you can retrain your brain and body to respond to your bedroom with sleepiness more quickly and automatically.

If you live in a studio apartment or have only a bedroom to yourself, it can be difficult to differentiate a space just for sleep. To train yourself to sleep in the bed, consider setting up your apartment or bedroom so there is a clear demarcation between your bed space and your living space. For example, you might arrange your furniture so your bed has its own space facing away from the rest of the apartment. You could use a curtain or place a piece of furniture so that the two spaces are more clearly separated.

Learn to Sleep Only in Your Own Bed

Do you nap or sleep anywhere other than your bed? If so, fill out the following contract and then stick with your commitments.

I'm likely to nap or fall asleep outside my bedroom _____, in the
(when)

_____ (room). To avoid this habit I will _____

Avoid Daytime Napping

For people with sleep problems, even a brief nap during the day can weaken the association between sleep and bed. When you fall asleep in places other than your bed, your body doesn't learn to relax and sleep when you enter your bedroom at night, which makes it difficult to get a good night's rest. Additionally, napping diminishes your ability to sleep at night.

Your need for sleep is limited. For example, suppose you need about seven hours of sleep each night. If you spend an hour napping during the day, this takes away time from the seven hours you might spend sleeping in bed at night. Getting your sleep all at once, in one block of time, is more restorative and refreshing than getting it in separate blocks of time.

If you absolutely must nap, be sure to do so before 2 p.m. and limit your naptime to twenty minutes.

When you are sleep-deprived, it might be important to recognize your sleepy times during the day and resist doing idle activities at those times (for example, watching TV or reading). One common example is sitting in a recliner after work and falling asleep. In this case, it might be important for you to stay busy after work instead of relaxing, to break the habit of napping.

♦ *How Donna Changed Her Napping Habit*

Donna often napped in her recliner after work while watching the evening news before eating dinner. If she were to continue to watch TV at this time, it would be difficult for her to avoid napping, because napping has become a habit.

But after noticing this pattern, Donna changed her routine. Now she goes through her mail while watching the news at the kitchen table. She is unlikely to fall asleep there. This small change eliminated a bad habit that was preventing her from getting a good night's rest.

Sleepy Times

You may be unaware of your sleepy times. However, it's important to understand your sleep pattern so you can avoid napping or falling asleep at times other than nighttime. Use the Energy Level Tracking Worksheet below to better understand your energy level throughout the day and identify your sleepy times. Choose a typical day and track your energy level hour by hour, using a scale of 0 to 10, with 10 being your highest energy level. You may want to take notes about what you were doing at that time. Also, it may be helpful to set an alarm to remind yourself to check your energy level every hour.

After charting your energy levels, you should have a good sense of when your energy dips. Review your Energy Level Tracking Worksheet and circle any sleepy times that you identified. These are the times that you may need to engage in an energetic activity to avoid the temptation to nap.

Try to schedule activities during these times that will help you avoid daytime napping, for example, stretching, taking a ten-minute walk, or meeting a friend at the gym. If your sleepy times are in the late afternoon, try not to use caffeine to stay awake, as you will need to stop consuming caffeine four or more hours before your bedtime (see chapter 5).

REDUCE HYPERVIGILANCE IN YOUR BEDROOM

Often people who have experienced a trauma develop an increased awareness of danger in the world. Before your trauma, you might have believed that bad things happen only to other people. Now you have a very real awareness that bad things can happen to anyone, including you. You may be more attuned to danger cues as a result of your experience, paying more attention to possible signs of danger and less attention to signs of safety.

It's true that a certain degree of watchfulness and caution makes sense for anyone. However, hypervigilance can be disruptive and can interfere with your recovery. Extreme watchfulness in your bedroom can keep you from taking back your bedroom for sleep.

Hypervigilance in the bedroom can take the form of:

◆ Placing weapons in your bedroom for protection

Mandy – 9/24/14

Energy Level Tracking Worksheet

Time	Energy Level (0 to 10)	Notes
6 a.m.	7	
7 a.m.	7	
8 a.m.	7	
9 a.m.	7	
10 a.m.	8	WALKED 2 MI
11 a.m.	9	
12 p.m.	10	MOWED LAWN
1 p.m.	10	
2 p.m.	9	
3 p.m.	9	VAC FLOORS
4 p.m.	8	
5 p.m.	~~8~~ 7	SUPPER ✓
6 p.m.	5	
7 p.m.	8	WATCHED TV BE BZ1SY
8 p.m.	7	
9 p.m.	5	
10 p.m.		
11 p.m.		
12 a.m.		
1 a.m.		

- Alerting and activating behaviors in your bedroom, such as listening for noises, looking around the room, or imagining something bad happening

- Getting up out of bed to check the locks or windows, and activities in and outside of the house

Excessive focus on danger cues in your bedroom gives your brain a sense of danger and alertness rather than a sense of calm, relaxed readiness for sleep. This makes it difficult to build a strong association between your bed and sleep.

Weapons

As a measure of protection, you may have placed a weapon in your bedroom after your traumatic experience. Military and police personnel may be accustomed to having a weapon with them at all times. You might believe that having a weapon nearby makes you feel more secure. Weapons may be guns or knives but may also include bats or other heavy objects intended for protection.

You will need to evaluate for yourself whether having a weapon in your bedroom actually does make you more secure. Use the following list to help you make this evaluation by circling true (T) or false (F).

Weapons in the Bedroom Evaluation	
I did not have a weapon in my bedroom before my traumatic experience.	T F
No one has ever broken into my home while I was asleep.	(T) F
There is at least a small chance that family members or friends could find my weapon and hurt themselves or someone else.	T (F)
Other people have expressed concern about my having a weapon in my bedroom.	T (F)
Sometimes when I awaken I'm groggy or disoriented for a few minutes.	T (F)
I've reached for my weapon when I thought I heard something and later realized it was nothing.	T F
When I hear a noise at night, I reach for my weapon, my heart races, and my muscles tense.	T (F)

If you answered true to one or more of these questions, you might want to evaluate whether it is worth it to you to keep a weapon in your bedroom. To use a weapon, you must be awake and alert. You can certainly awaken yourself quickly if you sense danger, but you will not be returning to sleep quickly. Thus, having a weapon in your bedroom is not compatible with the relaxation and calm needed for sleep.

You may want to try moving the weapon out of your bedroom to see if you sleep better. Although the thought of removing the weapon may seem overwhelming at first because of your post-trauma hypervigilance or your fear of being retraumatized, it is possible to do this slowly and gradually.

If needed, you can break the process down into manageable steps by gradually moving your weapon farther away from your bed until it is out of your bedroom. Choose how far you want to move it each time, recognizing that you may have some apprehension because it is not in its usual place. Use coping strategies such as calm breathing and self-talk to manage your anxiety. See chapter 4 for relaxation strategies to further manage and reduce your anxiety. Here are some examples of soothing self-talk.

- I am safe.

- Nothing bad is happening right now.

- I don't have to react to my feelings.

- I can wait and these feelings will pass.

- Add your own: _____

Use the following Weapon Removal Change Form worksheet to plan removing your weapons from your bedroom over a two-week period. Start gradually and move your weapon from its usual place in your bedroom to another place that is slightly farther from your bed. Understand that you may feel anxiety about not having your weapon close by, but if you persist in not moving the weapon back for several nights, your anxiety will diminish.

After the first move, once your anxiety has diminished, move the weapon again, just a little farther from your bed. Your goal is to move the weapon out of your bedroom. Repeat these steps as many times as it takes until you are satisfied with the location of the weapon outside of your bedroom. Once you've accomplished this, congratulate yourself on having achieved a very big step toward more restful sleep.

Weapon Removal Change Form

In order to sleep better, I want to remove _____N/A_____ (name of weapon) from my bedroom, which I keep _____ (name the place), to a location outside of my bedroom: _____ (name the place).

The current location of the weapon in my bedroom is: _N/A_____

Step 1: Move weapon from _____ to _____ in my bedroom.
 (current location in bedroom)   (Step 1 location)

Step 2: Move weapon from _____ to _____ in my bedroom.
 (Step 1 location in bedroom)   (Step 2 location)

Step 3: Move weapon from _____ to _____ in my bedroom.
 (Step 2 location in bedroom)   (Step 3 location)

Step 4: Move weapon from _____ to _____ in my bedroom.
 (Step 3 location in bedroom)   (Step 4 location)

Step 5: Move weapon from _____ to _____ , outside of my bedroom.
 (Step 4 location in bedroom)   (Final location)

DONNA'S WEAPON REMOVAL CHANGE FORM

Since her house was burglarized, Donna has slept with a gun in her bedside table and a kitchen knife under her bed. But now she has determined that having these weapons in her bedroom causes her to feel on guard in her bedroom. Furthermore, she recently was startled awake and grabbed her gun only to realize that her daughter had come into the bedroom. Donna decided that she must remove both of her weapons for better sleep and for increased safety. To help with this, she filled out and followed the Weapon Removal Change Form below, showing her plan for removing her gun.

Donna's Weapon Removal Change Form

In order to sleep better, I agree to remove _the gun_ from my bedroom, which I keep _in the bedside nightstand drawer_, to a location outside of my bedroom: _the hall closet gun safe_.

The current location of the weapon in my bedroom is: _bedside nightstand drawer._

Step 1: Move weapon from _bedside nightstand drawer_ to _dresser next to nightstand_ in my bedroom.
 (current location in bedroom)   (Step 1 location)

Step 2: Move weapon from _dresser next to nightstand_ to _chest next to closet_ in my bedroom.
 (Step 1 location in bedroom)   (Step 2 location)

Step 3: Move weapon from _chest next to closet_ to _bottom shelf of bedroom closet_ in my bedroom.
        (Step 2 location in bedroom)   (Step 3 location)

Step 4: Move weapon from _bottom shelf of bedroom closet_ to _top shelf of bedroom closet_ in my bedroom.
        (Step 3 location in bedroom)   (Step 4 location)

Step 5: Move weapon from _top shelf of bedroom closet_ to _hall closet gun safe,_ outside of my bedroom.
        (Step 4 location in bedroom)   (Final location)

Alerting and Activating Behaviors in the Bedroom

There is a difference between engaging in behaviors that keep you safe (vigilance) and behaviors that keep you safe but are either too excessive for the situation or are disruptive to other aspects of your life, such as your ability to sleep (hypervigilance). These hypervigilant behaviors, such as having a weapon by your bedside, disrupt sleep and keep you alert and awake. Your anxiety leads to thoughts and images of danger. Use your calm breathing and soothing self-talk to focus on the safety cues in your bedroom. Concentrate on the fact that in the present moment you are safe. Remind yourself that your internal alarm system is overly sensitive, making it difficult for you to distinguish between actual and perceived danger. Try using the soothing self-talk statements on page 42.

Responding to Noises

Resist the urge to get up and check every noise you hear when you are in your bedroom. If needed, you can use the Vigilance Checklist below to remind yourself that you have already engaged in safety activities and that checking them again would be an example of extreme watchfulness and would disrupt your efforts to reestablish bedroom cues as relaxing.

Use the Vigilance Checklist every night before bedtime until your desire to respond to noises diminishes. Describe the behavior you normally do at night to secure your home in the Vigilance Behavior column of the checklist. When you've completed the behavior, place an x under Completed.

When you've marked an x under Completed, it's important to resist the urge to do the activity again. Any urges to repeat the activity are examples of hypervigilance and should be avoided by using self-talk, calm breathing, or other distracting and soothing behaviors. Keep the checklist by your bed and if you have the urge to be overly vigilant, look at it.

Vigilance Checklist	
Completed?	**Vigilance Behavior**

Remember Donna from earlier in this chapter? Donna removed her weapons from her bedroom and used the Vigilance Checklist to fight her urge to be hypervigilant (by rechecking her home many times each night) before she could relax and fall asleep. See Donna's Vigilance Checklist example below.

Donna's Vigilance Checklist	
Completed?	**Vigilance Behavior**
x	Shed is locked.
x	Both cars are locked.
x	Back door is locked.
x	Front door is locked.
x	Windows in spare room are locked.
x	Window in bathroom is locked.
x	Gun safe is locked.

FOLLOW THE FIFTEEN-MINUTE RULE

Often, you may stay in bed when you're unable to sleep with the rationale "At least I'm resting" or "If I'm in bed long enough, eventually I'll fall asleep." However, these thoughts actually contribute to your insomnia. It's important that when you are in bed, you are sleeping, not awake and frustrated. Before your trauma, you likely took about fifteen minutes to fall asleep or return to sleep after awakening. Fifteen minutes is the approximate time it takes someone without sleep problems to initiate sleep. If you're not asleep within about fifteen minutes of lying in bed, get up out of bed. Sleep specialists Charles Morin and Colin Espie (2003) call this the fifteen-minute rule. Following the fifteen-minute rule will reteach your body to fall asleep when you get into bed.

1. Lie down in bed only when you're sleepy. Remain awake and out of bed until you feel drowsy.

2. If you're not asleep within approximately fifteen minutes after lying down, get out of bed and leave the bedroom. Go back to bed when you're feeling sleepy. Continue to get out of bed and leave the bedroom if you are not asleep after about fifteen minutes. Because you aren't looking at a clock in your bedroom anymore, you'll estimate when the fifteen minutes have passed. Practice the fifteen-minute rule even if you wake up in the middle of night and cannot return to sleep. Remind yourself that spending too much time awake in bed promotes insomnia and that you will be better off returning to bed only when you're sleepy.

3. Repeat the previous step as often as necessary throughout the night, until you are able to initiate sleep within fifteen minutes of getting into bed.

4. Before you go to sleep, plan what you will do and where you will go if you wake up during the night. For example, set up a chair in another room with some calming reading material or a relaxation tape, so if you get up during the night, it will be ready for you. Use these materials when you are awake at night to promote drowsiness. When you feel drowsy, return to bed.

Planning ahead what you will do when you get up at night means that you won't have to exert any energy thinking about what to do in the middle of the night. You can calmly go to your relaxing place and it will be ready for you. Promoting drowsiness is the sole purpose of your relaxing place. Stay there until you feel drowsy.

Pay attention to the signs that you may be ready to fall back asleep. These may include yawning or trouble keeping your eyes open. When you notice these signs, leave your relaxing place and return to bed. Use the My Relaxing Place Plan below to help.

Remember, the activities on your plan should include only those that promote relaxation and sleepiness since your goal is to fall asleep. Don't include any activities that expose you to bright light or require you to do a lot of thinking. Avoid watching television because it often contributes to your being awake and alert rather than relaxed.

My Relaxing Place Plan

- ◆ Read something that is relaxing or boring.

- ◆ Practice calm breathing (see above).

- ◆ Engage in a relaxation exercise (see chapter 4).

- ◆ Meditate.

- ◆ Drink warm milk or use another natural sleep aid.

- ◆ Listen to relaxing music.

- ◆ Do a jigsaw puzzle.

- ◆ Other: _____

Practice the fifteen-minute rule seven nights a week without exception. At first, following the fifteen-minute rule may be frustrating. It may be very difficult to get up out of bed when all you want to do is sleep. However, this is one of the most helpful strategies you can implement. Remember, your goal is to be in bed asleep. That's what drives the fifteen-minute rule. The longer you stay in bed awake, the more you weaken your association between your bed and sleep.

During the first week or so of implementing the fifteen-minute rule, you may have to get up several times a night and you may not get much sleep. However, as your sleep deprivation increases, it will be easier to fall asleep more quickly over the next several nights. Typically, forming a new sleep-wake cycle takes one to two weeks of practicing the fifteen-minute rule consistently every night.

Stick to your schedule and continue practicing these strategies even if you do not see any change immediately. Taking back your bedroom for sleep requires ongoing practice over some time. These skills need to be practiced every night as consistently as is possible.

UTILIZING SUPPORT

It is vital that you educate those who provide support to you during this part of your treatment. Engaging in important curative behaviors like the fifteen-minute rule can be disruptive to your partner's sleep. Working together to devise a time for you to start this part of treatment might help minimize some of the disruption and frustration.

Consider approaching your partner as soon as you finish reading this chapter and before you begin implementing the strategies. Explain that your sleep has been disrupted because of a disconnection between the bedroom and sleep, and although it may take some time to reestablish this connection and see improvement in your sleep, you will need your partner's assistance and support to be fully successful.

Be sensitive to your partner's needs. Many people without insomnia can watch television in bed and engage in other wakeful activities in the bedroom without experiencing any difficulty in their sleep. Perhaps this was true for you before your trauma. On the other hand, many partners would be happy to see weapons removed from the bedroom. Work with your partner to find ways that you can compromise.

For example, if your partner wants to keep the television in the bedroom, ask if it can be turned off by the time you are ready to go to sleep. You could also ask your partner to help you avoid daytime napping or sleeping outside of the bedroom by inviting you to engage in other activities during your daytime sleepy times.

Although the fifteen-minute rule is an important tool for eliminating insomnia, for your partner it may be the most disruptive tool. When you do get out of bed, be as quiet as possible to avoid awakening your partner. Wear slippers or socks rather than hard-soled shoes when you get up. If possible, avoid turning on any lights in or near the bedroom. Avoid making loud noises or engaging in activities that might disrupt your partner's sleep. If in spite of your best efforts your partner's sleep is still disrupted, consider asking your partner to sleep in another room temporarily.

Generally, the more you can help your partner understand the reasons behind the tools and strategies you are using, the more supportive he or she is likely to be, and the more successful you will be.

OVERCOMING OBSTACLES AND PLANNING FOR SUCCESS

You may find that the changes we suggest you make in this chapter are among the most difficult. For example, using the bedroom only for sleep many be contrary to what you've done for many years. It's common to want to avoid difficult practices, such as reducing hypervigilance in the bedroom and observing the fifteen-minute rule, because at first they can make you feel anxious or uncomfortable

To reach the long-term goal of improving your sleep, sometimes you must accept the shorter-term challenges of feeling anxious or even getting less sleep. It is of utmost importance that you not give in to these challenges. Extreme watchfulness in the bedroom is a key difficulty for many trauma survivors, and it turns the bedroom into a place for stress and anxiety rather than for calm, restful sleep. It is important to use the tools presented in this chapter to overcome hyper-vigilance in the bedroom.

Similarly, the fifteen-minute rule is central to overcoming insomnia and must be practiced faithfully to achieve a good night's rest. To help observe the rule, remind yourself that this technique, although difficult, is short-lived. In time, your body will relearn that the bed means sleep, and you will begin falling asleep more quickly and sleep for longer amounts of time. But meanwhile, if you're awake for longer than fifteen minutes, you'll have to go through the difficult process of getting out of bed each time. In the short run, giving up staying in bed awake will lead to long-term benefits. This will happen in a matter of weeks. Stick with it and you will earn the reward of sleeping soundly.

SUGGESTED GOAL ASSIGNMENT

You are well on your way to sleeping better. Use these goals to help improve your sleep even more:

1. Identify wakeful activities and move them outside the bedroom. Reserve your bedroom for sleep and sex only.

2. Limit your sleep to the bedroom. Do not sleep in any other room.

3. Avoid daytime napping, or limit a nap to one twenty-minute nap before 2 p.m.

4. Use the Energy Level Tracking Worksheet to identify the times of day that you are at risk for napping.

5. Reduce hypervigilance in your bedroom, including weapon removal, if needed.

6. Use the Weapons in the Bedroom Evaluation to decide whether having a weapon in the bedroom is a good idea for you, your family, and your sleep.

7. Follow the fifteen-minute rule every night and use your Relaxing Place Plan.

Chapter 4

Prepare Your Body and
Mind for Sleep

Being able to sleep requires a relaxed body and mind. Feeling tension in your body (physiological overarousal) or being emotionally upset (psychological overarousal) interferes with being able to fall and stay asleep. Going through a traumatic experience can leave you with an overamplified body and mind, and this feeling of being wired can prevent quality sleep.

Now you'll learn about the role relaxation plays in improving sleep and about several relaxation strategies, so you can begin practicing one that works well for you. You'll also learn strategies to deactivate your mind and relax your body, so you'll be on your way to better sleep. In this chapter you will:

- ◆ Learn the importance of relaxation in helping to improve sleep

- ◆ Learn and practice a relaxation exercise

- ◆ Learn a way to deactivate your mind at night

- ◆ Plan a bedtime wind-down routine

TRAIN YOUR BODY FOR SLEEP

Chapter 1 discussed how sleep problems can be due to the physical hyperarousal that often persists following a traumatic experience. To sleep, you must be able to reduce this bodily overarousal by relearning how to relax. Before your trauma, your body knew how to relax and sleep. Now using relaxation training to relearn how to relax is essential to being able to fall and stay asleep. It works by reducing the physiological and mental overarousal that was caused by your trauma. You cannot force yourself to sleep, but you can create optimal circumstances for a good night's sleep. Learning to relax, let go of tension, and decrease arousal is part of preparing yourself for good sleep.

Learning to relax your mind and body is a skill that takes time and practice. Set aside fifteen minutes every day during the daytime to practice at least one relaxation exercise. You may choose from the exercises below or choose another that appeals more to you. Make this a priority. Remember, you are practicing this exercise to improve your sleep.

Practice relaxing when you are awake and alert so you can learn what it feels like to be in a relaxed state. Also practice at night before you get into bed, to help your body and mind relax and prepare for sleep. Let's consider Joe's example.

◆ Joe's Story

Joe, a sixty-six-year-old businessman, was mugged at gunpoint while traveling in another city. Almost immediately after, Joe began having trouble sleeping in his hotel room. Soon, he noticed insomnia when he had to sleep anywhere away from home. He felt more alert and hypervigilant when traveling and began having problems relaxing. After several months, Joe began having problems sleeping at home. He was more irritable at work and in his personal life. When his wife noticed these changes, he realized he was having other signs of stress, including jaw clenching and tension headaches.

There are several important points in Joe's story:

- Experiencing a trauma changed Joe's sleeping pattern.

- He experienced emotional changes following his trauma, including increased irritability.

- Joe also observed physical changes after his trauma.

These emotional and physical changes and his insomnia are related to a generalized change in Joe's stress levels. Let's see how changes in your ability to relax can affect you.

Relaxation Training

Relaxation training includes several different strategies to learn to relax your body and mind and to become used to being relaxed while awake. This is important for two reasons:

1. Often, trauma survivors don't remember what it feels like to be awake and relaxed at the same time.

2. To be able to fall asleep, your body must know how to relax when awake.

Your state of physiological and mental arousal when awake may be much higher than it was before your traumatic experience or when compared to people who haven't experienced trauma. This hyperarousal makes you more reactive to stressful events. Learning how to relax and retraining your body will reduce your baseline tension level so that you are not as reactive nor as easily stressed. Examine the graph below.

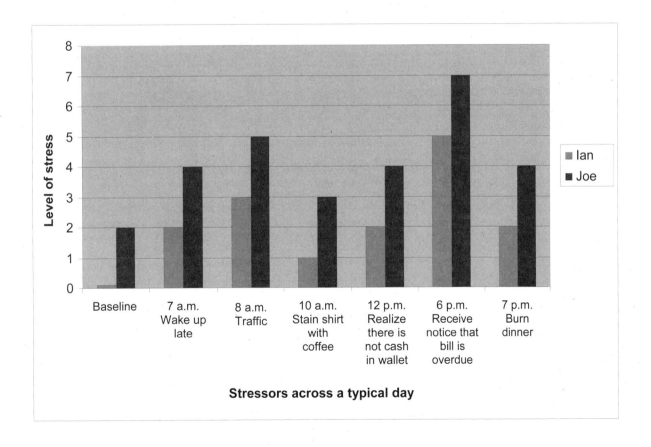

Ian never experienced a trauma. Joe is a trauma survivor. Joe's baseline level of arousal is higher than Ian's, even when no stressful events are occurring. Although the same events affect both Ian and Joe daily, who reacts more strongly? Why is this?

Ian's baseline level of arousal is lower than Joe's. Ian reacts to stressful events, but his reaction is likely to be less detrimental to his overall well-being than Joe's reaction is, because Joe is chronically overaroused. If Joe could bring his arousal level down to look more like Ian's, his stress reaction level would be lower, because his baseline stress level would be lower.

Relaxation training will lower your baseline arousal level and increase your ability to fall and stay asleep. If your body cannot relax, it will not sleep. Learning to invoke relaxation is essential to overcoming trauma-related insomnia.

To lower your arousal level, you must be able to be awake and relaxed. If you fall asleep during relaxation training, you'll teach your body to go to sleep but not to be awake and relaxed. Both tension reduction while awake and sleep facilitation at night are important goals of relaxation training. During the day, try to do relaxation training in an upright position to lessen the chance that you'll fall asleep when practicing. If you do relaxation training close to bedtime and become sleepy, discontinue the practice, get into bed, and let yourself fall asleep.

Sometimes when people begin practicing relaxation training, especially when anxious, they experience feelings that seem strange, mildly unsettling, and occasionally even anxiety provoking. Although this isn't typical, it's important to acknowledge it can occur occasionally and that it's normal. This reaction signals the state of your body is beginning to change. Usually, if this does occur, it will pass. Remember that you retain control at all times. If you feel you need to stop the practice, do so.

Instructions for three different relaxation training strategies appear below. You might want to try all three and choose the one that works best for you, or you may want to research other relaxation training strategies. The *Relaxation and Stress Reduction Workbook* (Davis, Eshelman, and McKay 2008) is a good source. Once you've found an exercise you like, set aside some time every day for practice. Even five minutes a day is a good start. Try building on your success and work up to fifteen minutes or more of daily relaxation training practice.

Consider using a recording of the instructions to help you practice. You might find recordings of such exercises online, or you can record yourself reading the instructions provided below into an audio recording device. Although using recorded or written instructions will help you learn these practices, your aim is to master the techniques so that you can practice without instructions. The more you practice, the quicker and more automatically you will be able to relax.

Progressive Muscle Relaxation

Progressive muscle relaxation (PMR) involves tensing and relaxing various muscle groups in your body sequentially. Tension in these muscles is associated with stress and anxiety, and release of tension is associated with relaxation. To achieve relaxation, focus on tensing each muscle group individually while keeping the rest of your body relaxed.

You'll flex or tense each muscle group for approximately ten seconds and then relax it for about twenty seconds. When you tense the muscle, try to create tension all at once rather than gradually. In the exercise below, use the word "now" as a cue to tense the muscles in the group you are working on all at once. The same applies to relaxing the muscles: release the tension instantly rather than gradually. Use the word "relax" as a cue to relax the muscles in the group you are working on all at once.

We will outline the PMR process first, then give you a script to follow as you practice this technique.

Start at the top of the list of muscle groups below. Use the description to the right of each muscle group for information about how to flex those muscles. Flex each muscle group at a tension level of 50 percent (do not strain) and then release it. Flex for ten seconds and then relax for twenty before moving to the next muscle group. Once you move to another muscle group, keep your other muscles in a relaxed state.

Notice the difference between the way your muscles feel when they are tensed and relaxed. This will help you recognize tension sooner so you can release it faster. While learning PMR, use the following script to help focus on tension and relaxation of the muscle groups in this exercise. Later, practice PMR without the script, or use the list of muscle groups as a cue for your practice. Skip any groups where you have an injury or pain.

Note: If you are concerned about flexing any muscles or doing PMR because of an injury or other health issue, try another relaxation strategy that is not a PMR technique. (See Self-Hypnosis and Autogenic Relaxation, below.)

Relaxation may be uncomfortable for you because of your overarousal. It can seem slow, boring, and even uncomfortable to relax. Try to remember why you are doing PMR: to improve your sleep. Try practicing PMR when you are already relaxed until you get used to doing it. This will help you master the technique.

As you get more comfortable relaxing, you can relax each muscle group for a longer time. That is, you can tense for ten seconds and relax for thirty seconds before moving on. You also can go through each muscle group twice. This will expand the amount of time you spend relaxing and increase your mastery.

The entire exercise should take you about eight minutes.

Muscle Group	Description
Fingers and hands	Tighten your hands into fists.
Forearms	Bend your wrists down or up.
Upper arms	Flex your biceps.
Shoulders	Lift your shoulders up toward your ears.
Right side of neck	Rotate your head to the right.
Left side of neck	Rotate your head to the left.
Neck and upper back	Tuck your chin to your chest.
Temple	Squint your eyes closed tightly.
Mouth and jaw	Open your mouth wide.
Upper back	Bring your shoulder blades together.
Chest	Take a deep breath that pushes your chest out.
Stomach	Tighten your stomach.
Lower back	Arch your back without straining.
Buttocks and thighs	Tighten your buttocks and thighs.
Legs and feet	Straighten and tense your legs and curl your toes downward.
Legs and feet	Straighten and tense your legs and flex your toes upward.
Whole body	Check each muscle group again and retense and relax any groups that are still tense. Continue to relax for a few minutes, noticing the sensation of relaxation in your body.

EXERCISE: Basic PMR Procedure

The following instructions are adapted from Davis, Eshelman, and McKay 2008, with permission from New Harbinger Publications.

Get into a comfortable position in a quiet room. Be sure all phones are off and that you won't be disturbed. Sit in a comfortable chair and take any other steps needed to ensure your comfort. You may want to remove your shoes or loosen tight clothing. Do nothing other than focus on this exercise.

Begin by taking slow, normal breaths in and out through your nose. Pause between breaths to slow down your breathing. As the rest of your body relaxes, create tension in the muscles of your hands by clenching both hands into fists now. Feel the tension in the muscles of both hands. Notice what it feels like as they tense and tighten. Hold the tension for about ten seconds…And relax. Notice what it feels like as the muscles of your hand relax. Let all the tension flow out of the muscles of both hands. Notice the difference between tension and relaxation in your hands. Focus on what it feels like as these muscles relax.

Now create tension in the muscles of your forearms by bending your hands backward at the wrist; do that now. As the muscles of your forearms tense and tighten, notice what that feels like. Feel the tension in the muscles of both forearms. Hold the tension for about ten seconds…And relax. Let go of all the tension in the muscles of your forearms. Notice what it feels like as these muscles relax. Let the muscles in your forearms smooth out and relax. Focus on what it feels like as these muscles relax. Notice the difference between tension and relaxation in these muscles.

Moving now to the muscles of your upper arms, create tension in the muscles of your upper arms by bending your arms and flexing your biceps now. Notice what it feels like as the muscles of your upper arms tense and tighten. Feel the tension in both upper arms. Hold the tension, and relax. Let go of all the tension in the muscles of your upper arms. Notice what it feels like as these muscles relax. Let the tension in the muscles of your upper arms just dissolve away. Focus on what it feels like as these muscles relax. Notice the difference between tension and relaxation in these muscles.

Moving now to the muscles of your shoulders, create tension in these muscles by lifting your shoulders up toward your ears now. Hold the tension. Notice what it feels like as the muscles of your shoulders tense and tighten. Feel the tension in your shoulders. And relax. Let go of all the tension in your shoulders. Notice what it feels like as these muscles relax. Let the muscles in your shoulders smooth out and relax. Focus on what it feels like as these muscles relax. Notice the difference between tension and relaxation in these muscles.

Moving now to the muscles of the right side of your neck, create tension in these muscles by rotating your head to the right now. Hold the tension. Notice what it feels like as the muscles of the right side of your neck tense and tighten. Feel the tension in the muscles of the right side of your neck. And relax. Let go of all the tension in the muscles of the right side of your neck.

Notice what it feels like as these muscles relax. Let the muscles in the right side of your neck smooth out and relax. Focus on what it feels like as these muscles relax. Notice the difference between tension and relaxation in these muscles.

Moving now to the muscles of the left side of your neck, create tension in these muscles by rotating your head to the left now. Hold the tension. Notice what it feels like as the muscles of the left side of your neck tense and tighten. Feel the tension in the left side of your neck. And relax. Let go of all the tension in the left side of your neck. Notice what it feels like as these muscles relax. Let the muscles in the left side of your neck smooth out and relax. Focus on what it feels like as these muscles relax. Notice the difference between tension and relaxation in these muscles.

Now create tension in the muscles of your neck and upper back by tucking your chin to your chest; do this now. Hold the tension in the muscles of your neck and upper back. Notice what it feels like as the muscles of your neck and upper back tense and tighten. Feel the tension in your neck and upper back. And relax. Let go of all the tension in the muscles of your neck and upper back. Notice what it feels like as these muscles relax. Let the muscles in your neck and upper back smooth out and relax. Focus on what it feels like as these muscles relax. Notice the difference between tension and relaxation in these muscles.

Moving now to the muscles around your eyes and temple, create tension in these muscles by squinting your eyes tightly; do that now. Hold the tension. Notice what it feels like as the muscles of your eyes and temple tense and tighten. Feel the tension in the muscles of your eyes and temple. And relax. Let go of all the tension in the muscles of your eyes and temple. Notice what it feels like as these muscles relax. Let the muscles in your eyes and temple smooth out and relax. Focus on what it feels like as these muscles relax. Notice the difference between tension and relaxation in these muscles.

Now move your attention to the muscles of your mouth and jaw. Create tension in your mouth and jaw muscles by opening your mouth widely; do this now. Hold the tension in the muscles of your mouth and jaw. Notice what it feels like as the muscles of your mouth and jaw tense and tighten. Feel the tension in the muscles of your mouth and jaw. And relax. Let go of all the tension in the muscles of your mouth and jaw. Notice what it feels like as these muscles relax. Let the muscles in your mouth and jaw smooth out and relax. Focus on what it feels like as these muscles relax. Notice the difference between tension and relaxation in these muscles.

Moving your attention now to the muscles of your upper back, create tension in these muscles by bringing your shoulder blades together; do that now. Hold the tension. Notice what it feels like as the muscles of your upper back tense and tighten. Feel the tension in the muscles of your upper back. And relax. Let go of all the tension in the muscles of your upper back. Notice what it feels like as these muscles relax. Let the muscles in your upper back smooth out and relax. Focus on what it feels like as these muscles relax. Notice the difference between tension and relaxation in these muscles.

Moving now to the muscles of your chest, create tension in these muscles by taking in a deep breath and holding it now. Hold the tension in the muscles of your chest. Notice what it feels like as the muscles of your chest tense and tighten. Feel the tension in the muscles of your chest.

And relax. Then breathe out and breathe normally again. Let go of all the tension in the muscles of your chest. Notice what it feels like as these muscles relax. Let the muscles in your chest smooth out and relax. Focus on what it feels like as these muscles relax. Notice the difference between tension and relaxation in these muscles.

Now move your attention to the muscles of your stomach. Create tension in the muscles of your stomach by tightening the muscles of your stomach, making them hard, as if you are preparing for a punch; do this now. Hold the tension in the muscles of your stomach. Notice what it feels like as the muscles of your stomach tense and tighten. Feel the tension in the muscles of your stomach. And relax. Let go of all the tension in the muscles of your stomach. Notice what it feels like as these muscles relax. Focus on what it feels like as these muscles relax. Notice the difference between tension and relaxation in these muscles.

Moving now to the muscles of your lower back, create tension in these muscles by arching your back without straining; do this now. Hold the tension in the muscles of your lower back. Notice what it feels like as the muscles of your lower back tense and tighten. Feel the tension in the muscles of your lower back. And relax. Let go of all the tension in the muscles of your lower back. Notice what it feels like as these muscles relax. Let the muscles in your lower back smooth out and relax. Focus on what it feels like as these muscles relax. Notice the difference between tension and relaxation in these muscles.

Now move your attention to the muscles of your buttocks and thighs. Create tension in the muscles of your buttocks and thighs by tightening these muscles now. Hold the tension in the muscles of your buttocks and thighs. Notice what it feels like as these muscles tense and tighten. Feel the tension in the muscles of your buttocks and thighs. And relax. Let go of all the tension in the muscles of your buttocks and thighs. Notice what it feels like as these muscles relax. Let the muscles in your buttocks and thighs smooth out and relax. Focus on what it feels like as these muscles relax. Notice the difference between tension and relaxation in these muscles.

Moving now to the muscles of your legs and feet, create tension in these muscles by straightening and tensing your legs and curling your toes downward now. Hold the tension in the muscles of your legs and feet. Notice what it feels like as the muscles of your legs and feet tense and tighten. Feel the tension in the muscles of your legs and feet. And relax. Let go of all the tension in the muscles of your legs and feet. Notice what it feels like as these muscles relax. Let the muscles of your legs and feet smooth out and relax. Focus on what it feels like as these muscles relax. Notice the difference between tension and relaxation in these muscles.

Now take a few minutes to enjoy the pleasant feelings of relaxation throughout your body. Moving back up your body, check for any remaining tension or tension that may have returned in any muscle group. If you notice tension, briefly tense and release that muscle group until the last bit of tension is gone. Let yourself become more and more deeply relaxed. Notice what it feels like to have your body so deeply relaxed. Focus on the feelings of calm relaxation. Continue to breathe slowly, breathing more deeply and slowly as you continue to relax. Your entire body is calm and relaxed.

EXERCISE: Short Basic PMR Procedure

Once you've mastered the basic PMR procedure, you can use the following shorter procedure. (Adapted from Davis, Eshelman, and McKay 2008, with permission from New Harbinger Publications).

1. Curl both fists and tighten biceps and forearms. Relax.

2. Roll your head around in a complete circle. Begin by pointing your chin toward your chest, then roll your head to the right, back, left, and down to your chest again. Then reverse. Relax.

3. Wrinkle up the muscles of your face all at once by wrinkling your forehead, squinting your eyes, opening your mouth, and hunching up your shoulders. Relax.

4. Bring your shoulder blades together while you take in a deep breath. Hold it. Relax.

5. Take another deep breath and push out your stomach. Hold it. Relax.

6. Straighten your legs and pull your toes up toward your face. Hold. Relax.

7. Straighten your legs and curl your toes down while tightening your calves, thighs, and buttocks. Hold it.

8. Relax.

Self-Hypnosis

When most people think of hypnosis, they may think of television shows where people are prompted to cluck like chickens or engage in other silly behaviors after visually following a moving object. These shows are entertaining but do not depict true hypnosis. *Self-hypnosis* uses the power of suggestion to help you become deeply relaxed. You can also use positive thoughts and images to relax and reduce stress.

It's likely that you've experienced a hypnotic state without knowing it. Have you ever driven a familiar road and suddenly realized you can't remember certain parts of the trip? Driving on automatic pilot is an example of a narrowing of consciousness similar to what happens in hypnosis. Self-hypnosis is effective for sleep disturbance, chronic pain, and anxiety management.

Set aside fifteen minutes once a day to practice self-hypnosis, and be sure to practice in a private place without interruption. Sit in a comfortable chair that supports your whole body. Recliners or high-backed chairs are perfect for relaxation practice.

EXERCISE: Self-Hypnosis

For this exercise you will go down an imaginary staircase to visit your special place in your imagination. Think about what that special place will be for you. It might be somewhere you've actually been and found relaxing and peaceful, or it might be a place you only imagine. For example, you could imagine lying on a beach, being in a meadow, or being in your room at home. You should feel secure and peaceful in your special place. In this self-hypnosis exercise, you're asked to use your imagination to experience all the sensations of your special place (sights, sounds, smells, touch, even taste may be included).

Here is a self-hypnosis script adapted from *The Relaxation and Stress Reduction Workbook* (Davis, Eshelman, and McKay 2008). Try recording this script and playing it back to help with the practice at first. Speak in a slow, even tone and pause between sentences.

Get into a comfortable position in a quiet room. Be sure that all phones are off and that you won't be disturbed. Sit in a comfortable chair and take any other steps needed to ensure your comfort.

Uncross your arms and legs. Do nothing other than focus on this exercise. Focus your eyes gently on a point in front of you. Take a deep, relaxing breath, letting the air go all the way to the bottom of your lungs, down into your abdomen. Take another slow, deep, relaxing breath… and another… Even though your eyelids are getting heavy and tired, keep your eyes open a little longer. Take another deep, relaxing breath…and another…and another.

Your eyes are becoming heavier and heavier… Let them close as you say to yourself, "Relax"… Now begin to relax all the muscles in your body. Starting with your legs, let your legs begin to relax… Your legs begin to feel heavy…heavier and heavier as they relax… Your legs are becoming heavier and heavier as they let go of the last bit of muscle tension… Your legs are becoming more and more relaxed, heavy and relaxed… Your arms, too, are becoming heavier and heavier as they let go of the last bit of muscle tension. You can feel gravity pulling your arms and legs down into the chair. You feel your arms growing heavier and heavier, more and more deeply relaxed… Your arms are letting go…letting go…letting go of tension as they become heavier and heavier…more and more deeply relaxed. Your arms and legs feel heavy and relaxed, heavy and relaxed. Your arms and legs feel totally relaxed as they let go of the last bit of muscle tension…

And your face, too, begins to relax. Your forehead is becoming smooth and relaxed, smooth and relaxed. Your forehead is letting go of tension as it becomes more and more smooth and relaxed, smooth and relaxed. And your cheeks, too, are becoming relaxed. Your cheeks are becoming smooth and relaxed, letting go of muscle tension and becoming smooth and relaxed. Your forehead and your cheeks are totally relaxed, smooth and relaxed. And now your jaw begins to relax… Your jaw is feeling loose and relaxed…loose and relaxed. As your jaw becomes more and more deeply relaxed, feel the muscles letting go of the last bit of muscle tension. And as your jaw becomes relaxed, your lips begin to part and your mouth falls open as your jaw loosens and relaxes…

Now your neck and shoulders begin to relax. Your neck and shoulders are loose and relaxed...loose and relaxed. Your shoulders are relaxed and drooping...relaxed and drooping. You feel your neck and shoulders becoming more and more deeply relaxed...loose and relaxed. Now take another deep breath in, and as you breathe out, let the relaxation spread into your chest, stomach, and back...

Take another deep breath, and as you breathe out, feel yourself becoming calm and relaxed, calm and relaxed. Feel yourself drifting deeper and deeper...deeper and deeper...drowsy and drifting, drifting and drowsy, becoming more and more drowsy, calm, and relaxed...drowsy, calm, and relaxed. Drifting and drowsy...drowsy and drifting...drifting down, down, down, into total relaxation...drifting deeper and deeper...deeper and deeper.

Now it's time to go to your special place, a place of safety and peace. Walk toward the stairway to your special place, and with each step down, count backward from 10 to 0, becoming more and more deeply relaxed with each step. In ten steps you will be there...feeling peaceful, safe, and calm... feeling more and more relaxed with each step... ten...nine...eight...seven...six...five...four... three...two...one... Now you are in your special place. See the colors and shapes of your special place... Hear the sounds... Smell the smells... See it... Feel it... Hear it... You can feel safe, peaceful, and calm in your special place...safe, peaceful, and calm. Feel yourself drifting deeper and deeper, deeper and deeper...more and more drowsy, peaceful, and calm... You feel yourself drifting deeper and deeper, more and more drowsy, peaceful, and calm...drifting down, down, into total relaxation. You are relaxed, peaceful, and calm. Take a few minutes to enjoy your special place....

Now, when you're ready, it's time to come back up the stairs, feeling alert, refreshed, and wide awake...alert, refreshed, and wide awake. Starting to come up now...one...two...three... four...five...six...seven...eight...nine... Begin opening your eyes...and ten...completely alert, refreshed, and wide awake...alert, refreshed, and wide awake.

Autogenic Relaxation

Autogenic relaxation uses suggestions of warmth and heaviness in your body to create a relaxed state. Similar to self-hypnosis, autogenic relaxation relies on suggestion to create a deep state of relaxation. Similar to PMR, it covers various muscle groups but does not require active tensing or releasing. As with other relaxation strategies, it's best to set aside time to practice in a quiet place without interruption; fifteen to thirty minutes a day is ideal. Practice in a comfortable chair that supports your head, back, arms, and legs. Or you can practice while lying on your back with your head supported and your legs about eight inches apart. The script below is also adapted from Davis, Eshelman, and McKay 2008, with permission from New Harbinger Publications.

EXERCISE: Autogenic Relaxation

Assume a comfortable position in a quiet room. Be sure that all phones are off and that you won't be disturbed. Do nothing other than focus on this exercise. Sit in a comfortable chair or lie down. Take other steps as needed to ensure your comfort. Scan your body to be sure you are in a tension-free position. Close your eyes if you feel comfortable doing so. Or pick a spot in front of you to focus on. Start by taking a few slow, relaxing breaths. Now, say these words to yourself

"My right arm is heavy and warm… My right arm is heavy and warm… My right arm is heavy and warm… I am calm and relaxed… I am calm and relaxed… I am calm and relaxed… My left arm is heavy and warm… My left arm is heavy and warm… My left arm is heavy and warm… I am calm and relaxed… I am calm and relaxed… I am calm and relaxed… Both of my arms are heavy and warm… Both of my arms are heavy and warm… Both of my arms are heavy and warm… I am calm and relaxed… I am calm and relaxed… I am calm and relaxed… My right leg is heavy and warm… My right leg is heavy and warm… My right leg is heavy and warm… I am calm and relaxed… I am calm and relaxed… I am calm and relaxed… My left leg is heavy and warm… My left leg is heavy and warm… My left leg is heavy and warm… I am calm and relaxed… I am calm and relaxed… I am calm and relaxed… Both of my legs are heavy and warm… Both of my legs are heavy and warm… Both of my legs are heavy and warm… I am calm and relaxed… I am calm and relaxed… I am calm and relaxed… When I open my eyes, I will feel refreshed and alert."

After the exercise, open your eyes and take a few deep breaths. Stretch your arms and legs and slowly return your body to an active state.

TRAIN YOUR BRAIN FOR SLEEP

There is no way for you to force yourself to sleep. Instead, you have to cue your brain to learn when and where to become sleepy, using both internal and external sleep cues. In this section, we will cover two strategies for modifying internal and external cues that will train your brain for sleep. Internal cues can be images, thoughts, or worries that might come up before sleep. External cues can be related to your environment or activities you do before sleep.

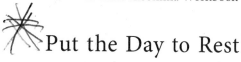

Put the Day to Rest

Do you tend to lie in bed with thoughts racing through your mind? Do you feel that you can't turn off your mind and that your thoughts keep you awake at night? Often, people with sleep problems cannot "shut down" when they get into bed, and as a result, they have trouble falling asleep. If this is true for you, here's a technique to help you put your day to rest (adapted from Morin and Espie 2003, with kind permission from Springer Science and Business Media).

EXERCISE: Put Your Day to Rest

1. Make copies of the Put the Day to Rest Worksheet

2. Early in the evening, in a different room than your bedroom, take a few minutes to think about your day.

3. Use the Put the Day to Rest Worksheet to write down any concerns or worries from your day.

4. Anticipate what might come to mind when you are in bed tonight and write it down.

5. Write out a brief plan of action (a to-do list) for tomorrow for how you might deal with each concern.

6. At bedtime, make sure that you've put this book and your Put the Day to Rest Worksheet in a room other than your bedroom. Remind yourself that you've already dealt with your worries and concerns.

7. If new thoughts come up, leave your bedroom and write them on your Put the Day to Rest Worksheet.

8. When you return to your bed, focus on positive thoughts and memories.

Put the Day to Rest Worksheet

Below, write down your worries or concerns left over from the day. These might be worries from the previous week or month, or concerns about today, tomorrow, or the future. These should be everyday concerns or worries that typically disrupt your sleep. Then write out a brief plan of action for how you might deal with each worry or concern.

Worry or Concern	Plan of Action/To-Do List
From the past	
From today	
For the future	
Other	

Bedtime Wind Down

Develop a bedtime wind-down routine to get into the habit of relaxing and preparing for sleep at the same time and in the same way every night. Using the same relaxing routine every night in the hour or two before bedtime will train your brain to expect sleep to follow. This means choosing one or two relaxing activities and doing them in the same order at the same time every night. Use the examples below (adapted from Morin and Espie 2003, with kind permission from Springer Science and Business Media) to choose activities you find relaxing, or you can think of some activities that aren't listed.

Relaxation-Promoting Activities

- Take a warm (not hot) bath or shower

- Drink a warm glass of milk

- Do some light reading (seated in a comfortable chair)

- Listen to relaxing music

- Practice calm breathing

- Practice a relaxation exercise

- Meditate or pray

Now use the worksheet below (adapted from Morin and Espie 2003) to develop your own bedtime wind-down routine. Think about:

- What you have to do before bedtime

- What activities you can do to promote relaxation

Do the things you must do first, such as household chores, and then start your relaxation wind-down. Be sure to start your routine early enough so that you don't feel rushed. Rushing is not relaxing.

Bedtime Wind-Down Routine

Choose activities that will cue you to relax and become sleepy. Remember to choose activities you can do every night in the same way. Be sure to give yourself enough time to complete these, so you don't rush.

Time	Activity

Here is Joe's completed bedtime wind-down routine:

Bedtime Wind-Down Routine

Choose activities that will cue you to relax and become sleepy. Remember to choose activities you can do every night in the same way. Be sure to give yourself enough time to complete these, so you don't rush.

Time	Activity
8:30 p.m.	Put the Day to Rest exercise
9 p.m.	Lock up house
9:15 p.m.	Take a warm bath and change into bedclothes
9:45 p.m.	Read
10:00 p.m.	Practice relaxation exercise
10:30 p.m.	Retire to bed and practice calm breathing

First, Joe did household activities that he felt needed to be done before he could relax. He then took time to put the day to rest, writing down his worries and concerns from the day and a to-do list for tomorrow. Then he secured his home, bathed, and changed into nightclothes (pajamas or clothes used only for sleeping), followed by reading for relaxation. After he finished these activities, he practiced progressive muscle relaxation. When he got sleepy anytime after 10:30 p.m., he got into bed and practiced calm breathing until he was able to fall asleep.

It's important for you to develop your own wind-down routine, which will cue your brain that the day has been put to rest and it is time for relaxation and sleep. Developing this routine will help you to prepare yourself for a good night's rest.

Choose Your TV Wisely

For some people, watching TV is a part of relaxing. As you learned in chapter 3 (and as we'll discuss further in chapter 5), it's important that you not watch TV in your bedroom. However, it also is important to monitor what you watch on TV before bedtime. TV can be provocative or arousing, causing you to think about issues or to get excited before bedtime. Such excitement conflicts with your strategy of trying to relax to induce sleep.

News programs are a good example of TV shows likely to be detrimental to your ability to relax. Many news programs follow the motto "If it bleeds, it leads" to capture their audience's attention. Consequently, much of the news is arousing if not downright upsetting. Having experienced a trauma can make watching these programs even riskier because the content might trigger traumatic memories. If a TV show or news program reminds you of your traumatic experience shortly before bedtime, this could put you into a heightened state of arousal that will interfere with your sleep.

Therefore, it is important to eliminate arousing TV shows and news programs from your late-night routine. If you must watch the news at night, do so before you start your wind-down routine. If you can limit watching the news to your morning routine, that would be even better.

UTILIZING SUPPORT

One of the best ways to learn a technique is to teach it to others. It will be helpful—and fun—if you learn the relaxation techniques and then teach them to someone else. Practicing with another person also can help you to stay on schedule for mastering the relaxation techniques. Try practicing with your partner before bedtime.

The decision of what to watch on TV definitely affects your partner. Discuss your plans for sleeping better with your partner and explain the rationale for choosing your TV programs wisely. Talk about the effect that these programs have on your mood and ability to sleep well at night.

Your partner or other family members may be more supportive and less likely to complain about TV restrictions when they understand how important this is for your health.

Finally, many people share household responsibilities in the evenings with a significant other. The bedtime wind-down routine needs to fit into both your schedule and your partner's. Discuss your bedtime wind-down routine with your partner.

OVERCOMING OBSTACLES AND PLANNING FOR SUCCESS

Time management is the largest obstacle encountered for the skills discussed in this chapter. Finding time to relax and finding time to engage in bedtime wind-down activities can be a challenge. Utilizing your support system and making these skills a part of your routine will help you overcome this obstacle. Consider setting an alarm to remind you to start your wind-down activities.

Changing TV habits is also challenging, especially when other family members have no difficulties watching late-night news or other programming. Remember that taking a break from stressful TV news and other such programming is good for your health.

SUGGESTED GOAL ASSIGNMENT

1. Practice relaxation training using the strategy of your choice for fifteen minutes or more each day. Practice during the day when awake and at night as part of your wind-down routine.

2. Put the day to rest early every evening in a different room than your bedroom.

3. Practice your bedtime wind-down routine every night at the same time.

4. Avoid late-night TV or other media that arouses you in any way.

Chapter 5

Help Yourself to a Good Night's Sleep

This chapter focuses on lifestyle and the habits that cause or maintain insomnia. You'll learn what these habits are and how to eliminate them. It also will introduce behaviors you can begin practicing to increase your ability to sleep better. In this chapter you will:

- Identify habits and preferences that may interfere with your sleep

- Identify features in your bedroom that may interfere with your sleep

- Begin to change the habits and the environment that prevent you from sleeping well

Consider Kristen's example.

◆ *Kristen's Story*

One night, Kristen, age fifty-one, got up to go to the bathroom. She didn't turn on the light, for fear of waking her husband. In the hallway, she slipped on her grandson's toy. She tried to break her fall but couldn't, and fell down the stairs. Kristen's legs were temporarily immobilized due to a spinal cord injury, and her calls for help went unheard until her husband awakened in the morning. She was unsure if she was bleeding internally or externally because of the dark and her inability to move. During this time, she believed that she would die.

Following her fall, Kristen had problems sleeping. These began because of her physical discomfort, but even after she healed, she continued having problems. She began to sleep with a night-light and then a hall light, and finally she left her TV on. After a poor night's rest, she drank more coffee in the morning to wake up. During her recovery from her injuries, she got out of the habit of exercising, and when she had healed, she never resumed it. She also began to smoke cigarettes again, after having quit for years. When awake at night, she found that smoking was emotionally relaxing and passed the time.

There are several important points in Kristen's story:

◆ She changed her bedroom environment in ways meant to help her sleep (keeping the light and TV on), but they actually contributed to her insomnia.

◆ After her trauma, Kristen developed habits meant to help her cope with sleepiness (increased caffeine intake), but they actually contributed to her insomnia.

◆ She also began engaging in behaviors meant to cope with frustration and other emotions, but they worsened her sleep problems (nicotine use).

HABITS AND PREFERENCES THAT INTERFERE WITH SLEEP

Your routine activities and behaviors that have become habits may contribute to your sleep problems. Similarly, your bedtime preferences could disrupt your sleep. You may be unaware that these behaviors interfere with sleep, or you may not fully understand the extent to which they interfere. You may have engaged in some of these behaviors before you had sleep problems. Others may have developed as a way to cope with trauma or trauma-related insomnia.

Unfortunately, some of the things you did before you developed a sleep problem may have to be reduced or eliminated now that you have sleep difficulties. This may not seem fair, especially because of changes you may have had to make since your trauma. Remember, although you may not be responsible for causing your sleep problems, you are the only one who can change them.

Here is a list of habits and preferences, or lifestyle factors, that contribute to sleep difficulties (adapted from Morin and Espie 2003). It's important to identify and change as many of these as possible so you aren't working against your goal to improve your sleep.

Do you...

- Use caffeine?

- Drink alcohol?

- Use nicotine?

- Eat large or heavy meals at supper?

- Rarely exercise?

- Use medications that increase alertness?

- Use sleeping pills?

If you answer yes to any of these, this chapter will help you improve your sleep.

CHANGING HABITS THAT DISRUPT SLEEP

Although initially your sleep problems may have resulted from going through a traumatic experience, certain habits may be maintaining your current sleep problems. Sometimes, the exact activities you engage in to cope with insomnia actually worsen it. Understanding this and changing these habits will improve your sleep.

Caffeine

Caffeine is a drug that can interfere with your ability to get a good night's sleep because it is a stimulant. *Stimulants* elevate heart rate and blood pressure and make you feel more alert, potentially adding to your overarousal and disrupting sleep. After a traumatic experience, you may feel more fatigued during the day. This fatigue can be related to sleep loss or to the stress of recuperating from trauma. Caffeine can give you a quick pick-me-up or help you stay alert throughout the day.

You may turn to caffeine in coffee, tea, or soda to help you manage fatigue and improve alertness. However, you may not realize that even moderate amounts of caffeine can affect sleep. Although there are individual differences in the stimulant effects of caffeine, it's important to consider the impact caffeine may have on your sleep.

Your body may have developed a tolerance to caffeine. That means your body is so used to caffeine that over time its impact has diminished, and you need more to get the same effect. For example, when you first started drinking coffee, one cup was all you needed to wake up in the morning. Now you may need three or four cups. Ingesting just 100 mg of caffeine per day—less than the amount in a single cup of brewed coffee—can lead to difficulty when discontinued.

Caffeine is also found in many other substances you may eat and drink. This includes hot tea, iced tea, soft drinks, energy drinks, chocolate, and some pain medications. For example, Anacin (aspirin), Excedrin (acetaminophen, aspirin, and caffeine), and Midol Complete (acetaminophen, caffeine, and pyrilamine) deliver between 32 and 65 mg of caffeine per tablet. If you are taking a pain medication, check with your health care provider or pharmacist to see if caffeine is an active ingredient.

ASSESS YOUR CAFFEINE USE

You may be unaware of the amount of caffeine in the foods you eat and drink daily. That makes it hard to estimate how much caffeine you ingest. Use the worksheet below to help you to get a rough estimate. It's likely you're a creature of habit and you consume about the same amount of caffeine every day. So tracking your intake for one to three days will allow you to see your pattern. Observe the total amount of your intake and the time you ingest your last caffeine each day.

Daily Caffeine Intake Tracking Worksheet

Substance	Single Serving Size	Estimated Caffeine Content	Serving Consumed Daily	Total from This Source	Time of Day Used
Brewed or drip coffee	8 fl oz	133 mg times no. of servings			
Espresso	1 fl oz	40 mg times no. of servings			
Decaffeinated coffee	8 fl oz	5 mg times no. of servings			
Brewed tea	8 fl oz	53 mg times no. of servings			
Bottled tea	16 fl oz	42 mg times no. of servings			
Cola	12 fl oz	35 mg times no. of servings			
Energy drinks	8 fl oz	80 mg times no. of servings			
Coffee ice cream	8 oz	68 mg times no. of servings			
Milk chocolate bar	1.5 oz	9 mg times no. of servings			
Dark chocolate bar	1.5 oz	31 mg times no. of servings			
Analgesics (e.g., Anacin or Excedrin)	1 tablet	65 mg times no. of servings			

I eat/drink a total of _____ mg of caffeine per day.

The time of my last caffeine intake is usually _____ p.m./a.m.

For example, Kristen always loved coffee. Before she fell, she drank one to two caffeinated beverages a day. After her fall, she started drinking increasing amounts of coffee, tea, and other caffeinated beverages to help her wake up after a poor night's sleep and to maintain alertness through the day. Several months after her accident, Kristen became aware that the quality of her sleep had deteriorated. Three to four nights a week, she had problems both falling and staying asleep.

After learning that caffeine could worsen her insomnia, Kristen decided to track her caffeine intake. Here is a copy of Kristen's worksheet.

Kristen's Daily Caffeine Intake Tracking Worksheet

Substance	Single Serving Size	Estimated Caffeine Content	Serving Consumed Daily	Total from This Source	Time of Day Used
Brewed or drip coffee	8 fl oz	133 mg times no. of servings	4	532	6 a.m. 10 p.m.
Espresso	1 fl oz	40 mg times no. of servings	0		
Decaffeinated coffee	8 fl oz	5 mg times no. of servings	0		
Brewed tea	8 fl oz	53 mg times no. of servings	10	530	4 p.m.
Bottled tea	16 fl oz	42 mg times no. of servings	0		
Cola	12 fl oz	35 mg times no. of servings	2	70	12 p.m. 6 p.m.
Energy drinks	8 fl oz	80 mg times no. of servings	0		
Coffee ice cream	8 oz	68 mg times no. of servings	0		
Milk chocolate bar	1.5 oz	9 mg times no. of servings	0		
Dark chocolate bar	1.5 oz	31 mg times no. of servings	0		
Analgesics (e.g., Anacin or Excedrin)	1 tablet	65 mg	0		

I eat/drink a total of *1,132* mg of caffeine per day.

The time of my last caffeine intake is usually *10* (p.m.)/a.m.

Kristen estimated that she consumed 1,132 mg of caffeine every day. Her intake came mostly from coffee and tea. Moreover, she found that she drank caffeine until late in the day. Because she had so much caffeine every day (well over the 100 mg that can lead to withdrawal symptoms), she decided to wean herself from it slowly to avoid withdrawal. You'll see later how she was able to do that.

ELIMINATE OR REDUCE YOUR CAFFEINE INTAKE

Some experts in sleep disorders recommend total elimination of caffeine from your diet; others say the effects are more variable and caffeine reduction can significantly improve sleep (Perlis et al. 2008). Headache is the most common withdrawal symptom from caffeine; it usually lasts twenty-four hours. More severe withdrawal symptoms can occur but are less common. These include fatigue, drowsiness, diminished ability to concentrate, diminished motivation for tasks, irritability, depressed mood, and nervousness, as well as some flu-like symptoms. These typically disappear within two days to one week. Unfortunately, when some people begin having these symptoms, they turn to caffeine to get rid of them, thus continuing the caffeine-dependence cycle.

If you have trouble reducing your caffeine intake or if you experience withdrawal symptoms while trying to eliminate it, do it more slowly, by reducing the number of caffeinated foods and drinks you use until you've eliminated them from your diet. Begin by reducing your main sources of caffeine slowly and eliminating minor sources.

It may be helpful to mix caffeinated and decaffeinated beverages to lower your risk of withdrawal. For example, use a mix of decaffeinated and caffeinated coffee or tea over a two-week period, slowly decreasing the percentage that's caffeineted, until you've totally eliminated caffeine from that source.

Look at Kristen's two-week caffeine reduction plan. Kristen drank about four cups of coffee every morning. Her plan was to totally eliminate coffee, a major source of her caffeine. She thought she could reduce her consumption of tea and minor caffeine sources without a reduction plan.

Kristen's Caffeine Reduction Change Worksheet

Caffeinated Substance: Coffee

Day	Percentage Caffeinated	Percentage Decaffeinated
1	75%	25%
2	75%	25%
3	75%	25%
4	50%	50%
5	50%	50%
6	50%	50%
7	25%	75%
8	25%	75%
9	25%	75%
10	25%	75%
11	0%	100%
12	0%	100%
13	Reduce number of cups from *3* to *2*	
14	Reduce number of cups from *2* to *1*	
15	Reduce number of cups from *1* to *0*	

Use the following worksheet to reduce your caffeine intake over the next two weeks.

Caffeine Reduction Change Worksheet

Caffeinated Substance:		
Day	**Percentage Caffeinated**	**Percentage Decaffeinated**
1	%	%
2	%	%
3	%	%
4	%	%
5	%	%
6	%	%
7	%	%
8	%	%
9	%	%
10	%	%
11	%	%
12	%	%
13	Reduce number of cups from _____ to _____	
14	Reduce number of cups from _____ to _____	
15	Reduce number of cups from _____ to _____	

Kristen chose to totally eliminate caffeine, which meant giving up decaffeinated coffee in addition to caffeinated, because decaffeinated beverages and foods still retain a small amount of caffeine. If this is your choice, look for products that state "caffeine-free" to be sure they don't contain caffeine.

The biggest barrier to reducing caffeine intake is our enjoyment of the foods and beverages that contain it. If you choose not to eliminate caffeine totally, it's important to have your last caffeinated substance four to six hours before your bedtime (see chapter 6 for strategies to set a bedtime). Use the Daily Caffeine Intake Tracking Worksheet to choose options that will reduce the amount you ingest. For example, switching from drinking 8 oz of drip coffee (133 mg) to 1 oz of espresso (40 mg) will reduce caffeine intake by 93 mg per serving.

If you are unsure whether caffeine negatively affects your sleep, limit or eliminate it for one to two weeks while tracking your sleep and see if it makes a difference. If you don't see a difference in the number of hours slept or the quality of your sleep, you may choose to resume your old caffeine intake.

Limit or Eliminate Alcohol

It isn't uncommon for people recovering from trauma to turn to alcohol to calm down, often to self-medicate to relax or to sleep. Alcohol can be sedating. Sometimes people turn to it to help numb the pain of remembering. Although this is understandable, alcohol is only partially effective and only in the short run. If you've tried it, you'll have noticed that in the long run, the memories and feelings remain and the negative effects of alcohol, especially on sleep, continue to grow.

Although alcohol may initially help you to relax and may even help you fall asleep at the beginning of the night, it will increase the number of times you awaken throughout the night. Even a small amount of alcohol as much as six hours before bedtime can increase wakefulness during the night.

Alcohol is a REM sleep suppressant (for a description of REM, see chapter 1). In the short run, you will fall asleep quickly and may even have fewer nightmares. However, in the long run, you'll experience increasingly fragmented sleep and frequent awakenings (Lamarche and De Koninck 2007).

Like caffeine and nicotine, alcohol is a drug that leads to tolerance so that people need more and more to get the same effect. This means, over time, more alcohol is needed to cause sleepiness or induce sleep. For people with heavy alcohol use in their past, even after years of abstinence sleep patterns may never completely return to normal.

Examine your Nightly Sleep Tracking Form (see chapter 2) and ask yourself if alcohol is related to the poorer quantity or quality of your sleep. If possible, eliminate alcohol use. Otherwise, limit its use by not drinking after dinner.

- ◆ Never use alcohol as a sleep aid. It only makes the problem worse.

- ◆ Never mix alcohol with other medications, especially sleeping pills.

If you are unsure whether alcohol affects your sleep or you want more information about how alcohol does affect your sleep, you can track how well and how much you sleep on nights when you do and don't use alcohol. The Alcohol and Sleep Tracking Worksheet below will help you examine your alcohol use.

To do Sleep Quality ratings related to alcohol, you'll rate your sleep each night on a scale of 0 to 10, with 0 indicating the worst sleep and 10 indicating the best quality sleep. You may want to judge this based on how rested you feel the next day or on how well you think you slept. Choose the rating method that seems best to you.

Alcohol and Sleep Tracking Worksheet				
Day	**Amount Used**	**Time of Last Use**	**Hours of Sleep**	**Sleep Quality**
Sunday				
Monday				
Tuesday				
Wednesday				
Thursday				
Friday				
Saturday				

Kristen wondered if her alcohol use impacted her sleep. Using the Alcohol and Sleep Tracking Worksheet for one week, she discovered that her alcohol intake, which was heavier Thursday through Saturday, clearly affected the quality of her sleep. She also found that even in small amounts alcohol was disruptive to a good night's rest.

Kristen's Alcohol and Sleep Tracking Worksheet

Day	Amount Used	Time of Last Use	Hours of Sleep	Sleep Quality
Sunday	None		5	6/10
Monday	2 drinks	11 p.m.	4	5/10
Tuesday	None		5.5	6/10
Wednesday	None		4.5	6/10
Thursday	4 drinks	11 p.m.	4	4/10
Friday	6 drinks	1 a.m.	3.5	2/10
Saturday	6 drinks	11 p.m.	4	2/10

If, like Kristen, you find your alcohol use is related to your sleep problems, it's important to reduce the amount you consume and how often you consume it. Occasional drinking may not be detrimental to your sleep pattern, while regular use is. If you want to reduce your alcohol intake but are unsure if you can or how to begin, there are resources available. Consult your physician or join a substance abuse group like Alcoholics Anonymous.

Limit or Eliminate Nicotine

Nicotine is another drug that interferes with sleep. Nicotine is present in tobacco products such as cigarettes, cigars, and chewing tobacco, as well as electronic cigarettes, nicotine patches, and gums. Smoking is often used as a coping strategy by people who've experience trauma (Acierno et al. 1996). Recently, researchers (Smith et al. 2008) found that the stress of military deployment was associated with people who had never smoked beginning to smoke, as well as with people who had quit smoking restarting. Notice whether your trauma reminders or feelings of stress trigger nicotine cravings, and if they do, plan alternative activities or coping strategies.

Nicotine products increase heart rate, blood pressure, and breathing rate and make you feel more alert. Nicotine also leads to tolerance, so that you need more to get the same effect. Serious physical health consequences are associated with tobacco and nicotine use, such as cancer (for example, lung, mouth, and throat cancers), heart attacks, stroke, and pulmonary problems.

Smokers sleep more poorly than nonsmokers due to the stimulating effects of nicotine. Many people think that smoking cigarettes relaxes them, but actually the nicotine in cigarettes is very stimulating and works against efforts to sleep. The relaxing part of tobacco use is the habit that is involved, and the key to quitting is to develop new habits.

Nicotine also interferes with sleep because smokers have nicotine withdrawal symptoms while asleep. When you are sleeping, your body begins to withdraw from nicotine, which can cause wakefulness. If you awaken during the night, your body will crave the drug, making it harder for you to return to sleep. Allowing yourself to use nicotine during these awakenings is disruptive because it is a wakeful activity, and because the nicotine will physically stimulate you. Both factors make it harder to return to sleep.

Smoking also interferes with sleep because of respiratory irritation. Smokers often breathe in a more labored way than nonsmokers. This can disrupt restful sleep.

Quitting smoking can be difficult because nicotine use leads to chemical dependence. Nicotine withdrawal symptoms include restlessness, difficulty sleeping, irritability, anxiety, and headaches. They usually last ten days. If you are not ready to quit smoking completely, cut down on nicotine at night:

- Stop smoking within several hours before bedtime.

- Don't smoke if you get up during the night.

- Try to reduce your nicotine intake during the day.

It would be helpful to track how nicotine affects your sleep. Use the Nicotine and Sleep Tracking Worksheet below to understand how nicotine affects the quality and quantity of your sleep.

Nicotine and Sleep Tracking Worksheet

Day	Amount Used	Time of Last Use	Hours of Sleep	Sleep Onset Estimate
Sunday				
Monday				
Tuesday				
Wednesday				
Thursday				
Friday				
Saturday				

Kristen wanted to quit smoking. Typically, she smoked a pack a day. On most nights, her last cigarette was a few minutes before bedtime. When she wanted to smoke, she had to go outside because she didn't smoke in the house. Kristen tracked her smoking to see if it was disrupting her sleep.

Kristen's Nicotine and Sleep Tracking Worksheet

Day	Amount Used	Time of Last Use	Hours of Sleep	Sleep Onset Estimate
Sunday	1 pack	11 p.m.	4	1 hour
Monday	¾ pack	11:10 p.m.	3.5	1.25 hours
Tuesday	1 pack	12 a.m.	3	1 hour
Wednesday	1¼ packs	10 p.m.	3	40 minutes
Thursday	¾ pack	11 p.m.	4	1 hour
Friday	¾ pack	9 p.m.	4.5	30 minutes
Saturday	¾ pack	9 p.m.	4.5	30 minutes

Kristen knew that she usually smoked her last cigarette just before bedtime. When she smoked her last cigarette later, she noticed that the time it took her to fall asleep was longer because of the stimulating effect of nicotine. The number of hours she slept was not affected by slight changes to the time of her last use or to the amount of nicotine she consumed. However, if she were to stop smoking or make larger changes to her nicotine intake, she might begin sleeping longer at night.

If you track the effect nicotine has on your sleep and find that it's detrimental, it will be important to stop smoking or reduce your nicotine intake. There are many resources to help you stop smoking. Consult your physician for a medication that blocks nicotine receptors and reduces cravings, such as Wellbutrin (bupropion). Use the patch or nicotine gum to reduce your use. There may be programs in your community that can help you quit. Check the resources section for help with finding programs in your area.

Manage Your Diet

Eating a large meal for dinner can make it harder to sleep at night. Try eating a smaller meal for dinner, and eat it at least two to three hours before your average bedtime. Avoid heavy, spicy, or high-sugar foods; they can interfere with sleep. If you get hungry between your last meal and bedtime, try a small high-carbohydrate snack. Carbohydrates are relaxing because they increase levels of serotonin, a brain chemical that plays a key role in mood and relaxation. A light snack, high in carbohydrates, such as bread, a bagel, or crackers might help you to relax.

Foods that may help induce sleep

- ½ bagel

- 2 slices of turkey

- 8 oz glass of milk (warm or cold)

- a small cup of chamomile or caffeine-free tea

It's also important to drink enough water. Stay well-hydrated because being dehydrated can reduce sleep quality. Be careful to reduce fluid intake after 7 p.m. so you aren't awakened by the need to urinate. On average, people need eight 8-ounce glasses of water each day.

You may need more or less depending on your lifestyle. People who are more active, live in dry or hot climates, exercise regularly, or ingest dehydrating substances (for example, caffeine) may need more water to remain hydrated.

Thirst is a sign of dehydration; if you are frequently dehydrated, you may need to increase your water intake. If you drink enough water each day but remain thirsty, speak to your physician about other reasons you may be dehydrated. Uncovering and dealing with medical issues that may contribute to dehydration could help your overall health and sleep pattern.

It may help to track how your diet affects your sleep. The meals that most affect insomnia are those eaten in the afternoon and evening. Track your diet for one week to see if what and when you eat is associated with your sleep difficulties.

To do Sleep Quality ratings related to diet, rate your sleep each night on a scale of 0 to 10, with 0 indicating the worst sleep and 10 indicating the best quality sleep you can get. You can judge this on how rested you feel the next day or on how well you think you slept. Choose the rating method that seems best to you.

For one week, record on the worksheet below what you ate during each hour for the six hours before you tried to fall asleep. Circle any large, spicy, or heavy meals you ate. At the end of the week, assess whether your sleep quantity or quality was poorer when you ate later or ate large, spicy, or heavy meals (indicated by circles on your worksheet).

Diet and Sleep Tracking Sheet										
	4 p.m.	5 p.m.	6 p.m.	7 p.m.	8 p.m.	9 p.m.	10 p.m.	11 p.m.	12 a.m.	Sleep Quantity and Quality
Sun.										___ hrs. ___ /10
Mon.										___ hrs. ___ /10
Tues.										___ hrs. ___ /10
Wed.										___ hrs. ___ /10
Thurs.										___ hrs. ___ /10
Fri.										___ hrs. ___ /10
Sat.										___ hrs. ___ /10

Promote Exercise

Exercise is good for sleep because it increases your metabolism, making your body perform more efficiently and increasing the need to sleep. People who are more active sleep better. Exercise may help you enter deep sleep faster and remain in these deep stages longer (Perlis et al. 2008). Moderate exercise helps people fall asleep faster and sleep longer (King et al. 1997). Exercise reduces the risk of developing many health problems and appears to decrease depression and anxiety symptoms.

Do thirty minutes of a moderate exercise routine every day, early in the day. Exercising later in the day may disrupt sleep (Morin and Espie 2003). If it's difficult to sleep after exercising in the evening or afternoon, chart whether the time you exercise is related to your ability to initiate sleep. The worksheet below can be used for this purpose. Although there is no evidence that one type of exercise is better for sleep than others, here are some ways to become more active to improve sleep.

Exercises and Activities to Promote Sleep

- Cardiovascular exercise

    - Walking, running, biking, swimming, or any other activity that raises your heart rate

- Strength training

    - Weight lifting, Pilates, yoga

- Physical activities

    - Gardening, housecleaning, painting, or other physical activities from your everyday life

Try to set up a regular exercise routine for the morning or early afternoon. Be sure to get your health care provider's permission first. Note that exercising within two to three hours before bedtime may make it harder to sleep.

Use the Exercise and Sleep Tracking Worksheet below to plan a better night's rest daily. Remember to exercise in the morning or early in the day because this is better for your sleep. Every day, write down the exercise you did and the amount of time spent in each activity. You may notice that some activities help you sleep better than others. If you do notice that one type of exercise (for example, cardiovascular) improves your sleep, you may want to add it to your routine more often.

Also, it might help to track the numbers of hours of sleep and your sleep quality ratings for the days that you do and do not exercise. This will show you that you do indeed have better sleep on days you do some physical activity. **Note:** You're more likely to exercise if you do something enjoyable or do it with another person.

If you do no exercise or activity, simply write, "None." Be sure to track your sleep quality and quantity even for days that you don't exercise.

Exercise and Sleep Tracking Worksheet				
Day and Time	Activity	Time Spent in Activity	Hours of Sleep	Sleep Quality Rating
Sunday _____ a.m./p.m. _____ a.m./p.m. _____ a.m./p.m. _____ a.m./p.m. _____ a.m./p.m.				_____/10
Monday _____ a.m./p.m. _____ a.m./p.m. _____ a.m./p.m. _____ a.m./p.m. _____ a.m./p.m.				_____/10
Tuesday _____ a.m./p.m. _____ a.m./p.m. _____ a.m./p.m. _____ a.m./p.m. _____ a.m./p.m.				_____/10
Wednesday _____ a.m./p.m. _____ a.m./p.m. _____ a.m./p.m. _____ a.m./p.m. _____ a.m./p.m.				_____/10

Thursday				____/10
____ a.m./p.m.				
____ a.m./p.m.				
____ a.m./p.m.				
____ a.m./p.m.				
____ a.m./p.m.				
Friday				____/10
____ a.m./p.m.				
____ a.m./p.m.				
____ a.m./p.m.				
____ a.m./p.m.				
____ a.m./p.m.				
Saturday				____/10
____ a.m./p.m.				
____ a.m./p.m.				
____ a.m./p.m.				
____ a.m./p.m.				
____ a.m./p.m.				

Here is an example of Kristen's worksheet. Note that Kristen's quantity differs from her quality of sleep. That is, sometimes exercise didn't make Kristen sleep more hours, but did improve her sleep quality rating or her feeling of being rested the next morning. Also, sometimes just a few minutes of activity improved her sleep.

Kristen's Exercise and Sleep Tracking Worksheet				
Day	Activity	Time Spent in Activity	Hours of Sleep	Sleep Quality Rating
Sunday *7 a.m.* *7 p.m.*	*Walking* *Doing dishes*	*15 min.* *5 min.*	*4*	*6/10*
Monday *6 a.m.* *6 p.m.*	*Jogging* *Laundry*	*10 min.* *120 min.*	*6*	*8/10*
Tuesday *6 p.m.* *7 p.m.*	*Jumping rope* *Ironing*	*5 min.* *20 min.*	*4*	*8/10*
Wednesday *7 a.m.*	*Walking*	*45 min.*	*5*	*8/10*
Thursday _____ a.m./p.m.	*None*		*5*	*3/10*
Friday *6 a.m.* *1-3 p.m.*	*Bike ride* *Took stairs at work (5 flights)*	*60 min.* *6 min. (2 times)*	*4*	*9/10*
Saturday _____ a.m./p.m.	*None*		*6*	*5/10*

MEDICATIONS AND SLEEP

You may be taking medications for physical or emotional problems. Some may be physically stimulating; that is, they may increase alertness or wakefulness and can contribute to your sleep problems. Physicians may prescribe these medications without screening patients for insomnia and may not realize that they interfere with sleep.

Stimulating medications are used to treat depression, high blood pressure, obesity, asthma, and cancer, among other medical conditions (Hauri and Linde 1996). The list below names some common medications that can interfere with sleep by causing or complicating insomnia (Hauri and Linde 1996; Perlis et al. 2008; Sandor and Shapiro 1994). Moreover, some drugs cause daytime sedation, which makes it difficult to be active or to resist sleeping during the day, thereby interfering with your ability to sleep at night.

Talk to your physician about alternative medications that will not disrupt sleep, or ways to take the medications that will be less likely to disrupt sleep (for example, take a sedating medication only at night). **Caution:** Do not discontinue or change the dosage of your medication without first consulting your physician.

Types of Medications That May Impact Sleep

- Amphetamines
- Antiarrhythmics
- Antidepressants
- Antiepileptics
- Antihistamines
- Antihypertensives
- Antiparkinsonian medications
- Appetite suppressants
- Barbiturates
- Beta agonists
- Benzodiazepines
- Bronchodilating drugs
- Decongestants
- Medications that contain caffeine
- Steroids
- Thyroid medications

SLEEPING PILLS

Today, sleeping pills get more press than ever. TV commercials promise a good night's rest with pills, if you just consult your physician. Also, many over-the-counter pills to aid sleep problems are widely available. Some medications prescribed for sleep were not designed as sleep aids but have the side effect of sedation. Most medications designed specifically for sleep are for short-term use only or to treat occasional sleep problems—not chronic ones.

Side effects. Sleeping pills have these side effects: daytime drowsiness, high blood pressure, dizziness, nausea, poor coordination, and restlessness, among others. Mixing sleeping pills and alcohol can be lethal. Alcohol is a depressant, and mixing it with sleeping pills can slow respiration and put your health at risk.

Rebound insomnia. The danger in taking sleeping pills for chronic insomnia is dependence, or what is called *rebound insomnia*. Once your system is accustomed to sleeping pills, ending their use can cause the insomnia to worsen. It can take several weeks to eliminate sleeping pills' effects from the body, so many people choose to continue taking them to avoid worsening their sleep problems.

Tolerance. Over time, sleeping pills wane in effectiveness for treating chronic insomnia. At first they work, for a few weeks to months, but their effect slowly fades. Taking the pills in higher dosages can help for a while, but eventually your body becomes accustomed to the higher dosage. By raising the dosage, you risk becoming more dependent on sleep aids. Taking sleeping pills can keep you from alleviating your sleep problems for good. The skills you'll learn using this workbook have no side effects, won't cause dependence, and will help you get a good night's rest.

Effectiveness. You know a sleep aid is working if while taking it (1) you fall asleep within fifteen to twenty minutes; (2) you sleep with only minor awakenings during the night; (3) you sleep enough hours to feel rested; and (4) you are not hungover, drowsy, or significantly fatigued the next day. If you are taking a sleep aid but not benefiting from it in these ways, discuss discontinuing the medication or limiting its use with your physician.

GOOD SLEEP AND YOUR ENVIRONMENT

Making small changes to your bedroom environment can improve your sleep. To ensure your surroundings are as conducive to sleep as possible, pay attention to the following environmental factors (adapted from Morin and Espie 2003):

- ◆ Noise

- ◆ Lighting

- Room temperature

- Air quality

- Bed comfort

- Clothing choices

Optimizing Your Sleep Surroundings

It's important to assess and change things in your bedroom environment that may contribute to or worsen your sleep problems. Your surroundings should promote good sleep.

LIMIT NOISE

It's common for bedroom noise to contribute to sleep problems after a trauma. There is great variability in the amount of quiet or noise people need to fall asleep. Some like a steady background noise to mask outside noises that might awaken them. Others sleep better in a quiet room. Evaluate your sleep preference and change your environment as needed. It may help to try quietness if you usually sleep with noise. If you usually sleep without any sounds, try white noise (monotonous, repetitive noise like that made by a fan, air purifier, or white noise machine) to see if this makes a difference. If you know your preference along the noise/no noise continuum, be sure your optimal sound level is achieved so you can sleep comfortably in your environment.

If you like having background noise, it's important not to use TV for this purpose. Leaving the TV on or falling asleep to the TV is bad for sleep for several reasons:

- Watching TV is a wakeful activity that should not be done in the bedroom (see chapter 3). It doesn't help you learn to associate your bedroom and bed with relaxation and sleep.

- TV sound varies in volume. TV commercials are often louder than the programs. This is done to get your attention—and it works. The louder segments will capture your attention while you are preparing for sleep and awaken you if you are sleeping; both affect the quality of your sleep.

- Falling asleep to the sound of TV delays sleepiness longer than if you learned to fall asleep without it. With TV, you may begin to feel sleepy, but then you begin attending to what's on TV. This delays sleep, and you may feel even less sleepy when the program ends. Learning to fall asleep without TV will help you to initiate sleep more effectively.

- Having the TV on in the bedroom often leads people with middle insomnia (waking in the middle of the night) to watch it rather than engage in an activity that would promote returning to sleep. In the same way that TV can keep you from falling asleep, it can keep you from returning to sleep after an awakening.

If you like background noise, it's best to choose a monotonous sound rather than a varying one. Try one of these options instead of the TV:

- Turn the radio on low and tuned in between stations.

- Use a fan.

- Use a white noise machine.

- Use a clock, metronome, or other soothing rhythmic noise.

LIGHTING

Be sure to get some exposure to sunlight every day, including early evening, if possible. This helps to regulate your biological clock. If you work indoors, try taking a break outside or take a walk when you return home in the evening to get exposure to sunlight.

At bedtime, keep the bedroom lighting low. At night, when you enter your bedroom, use a small lamp rather than a bright overhead light. This is part of the general strategy to make your bedroom soothing and associated with relaxation and sleep.

If you wake in the middle of the night to use the bathroom or to go into another room, use night-lights or other low-level lighting and avoid exposure to bright light. A bright light will signal your brain that it is time to awaken.

ROOM TEMPERATURE

Most people fall asleep faster and sleep better in a slightly cool room rather than one too warm. A too hot room leads to more awake time and light sleep. Think about your temperature preference. Most people like it to be about 70 degrees Fahrenheit. Make sure your bedding is comfortable and keeps you cool or warm enough.

AIR QUALITY

Improve the air quality in your bedroom by making sure it is well ventilated. If a room is too stuffy, it's harder to sleep. A fan can be used both to move air and as background noise, if desired.

BED COMFORT

Make sure your mattress and pillows are comfortable. After ten years' use, replace a mattress with the highest quality you can afford. When you buy a new mattress, test it in the store. Many mattresses are designed to be more comfortable for certain sleep positions than others. Ask your salesperson about the mattress design and lie on the mattress in your preferred sleeping position (the position you sleep in for longer periods of time) to be sure you're comfortable.

CLOTHING CHOICES

Sleep in pajamas or comfortable clothes made specifically and only for sleep. Don't wear a tee shirt to bed that you might wear in the daytime. Bed clothing should be different from clothes you wear when awake. This helps your body move into a sleepy mode. Make sure your clothes are not tight, which disrupts sleep. Also, be sure your clothing doesn't make you too hot or cold while sleeping.

UTILIZING SUPPORT

Your sleep problems affect your partner. Therefore, your sleep solution will also affect him or her. To sleep better, you must make changes to your lifestyle, behavior, and environment. This often means that your partner must make these changes too, even if he or she doesn't have sleep problems. You want your bedroom environment to be as comfortable as possible for both you and your partner. Making changes to your bedroom will require your partner's understanding and support.

The decision to remove the TV from your bedroom is an example of an area where you'll need support. It's important to talk to your partner about your reasons for wanting to move the TV out of your bedroom, because people who have no sleep problems may not be bothered by a TV in their bedroom and may even enjoy having it there and watching it with you.

Discuss your reasons for making these changes with your partner. Talk about the good effects your improved sleep will have (for example, you'll be less tired and irritable, and you'll want to engage in more activities). Discuss how this will benefit your relationship.

It's important to make sleeping better not just about you but also about your ability to be a productive member in your relationship, family, and work environment. Explain the reasons you're making these changes and share material from this workbook. That may strengthen your partner's support for your progress toward sleeping better. Use the following Environment and Sleep Compromise Worksheet to aid your discussion. If you need ideas on how to work with it, see Kristen's worksheet below

Environment and Sleep Compromise Worksheet

Environmental Factor	You	Your Partner	Compromise
Noise			
Light			
Temperature			
Bedding			
Air quality			

Kristen identified ways she wanted to change her bedroom environment to sleep better. She used the following worksheet to discuss these changes with her husband Bob.

Kristen's Environment and Sleep Compromise Worksheet

Environmental Factor	You	Your Partner	Compromise
Noise	Radio music	None	Fan
Light	Closet light on	None	Night-light
Temperature	65	75	70
Bedding	Sheet and light blanket	Sheet and heavy blanket	Light blanket on the whole bed and a heavy throw just for Bob
Air quality	Fan	None	Fan

Bob realized he wanted Kristen to sleep better and understood that this would affect the quality of life for both of them. He didn't want to negatively impact his own sleep but was willing to compromise. By working together they were able to arrange their bedroom so they both get a good night's rest.

OVERCOMING OBSTACLES AND PLANNING FOR SUCCESS

Making changes to your lifestyle and environment can be difficult. It's common to want to sleep better but not want to make these changes to achieve better sleep. Also, you may be hesitant to ask your partner to make changes, or you may meet resistance when trying to implement changes that affect your partner.

To overcome these obstacles, it's important to ask yourself how poorly you sleep and what it's worth to you to sleep better. How will your sleeping better affect your significant other? How will sleeping better affect other important parts of your life, such as at work or school, or your friendships, self-esteem, and mood?

As stated in chapter 1, if you have chronic trauma-related insomnia, it is unlikely to go away on its own. To recover, you must implement lifestyle and environmental changes. After you've been sleeping better for several months, you may choose to resume some of your old habits. If you decide to do this, it will be important for you to use the Nightly Sleep Tracking Form from chapter 2 to track the quality and quantity of your sleep and see how they are affected by your lifestyle or environmental choices. If you notice, for example, that reintroducing TV to your bedroom disrupts your sleep, you can remove that habit from your life once again. Nevertheless, at the present time, certain changes must be made to overcome your current sleep problems.

SUGGESTED GOAL ASSIGNMENT

1. Continue to add to your successes. Identify and change habits and preferences that interfere with sleep, including:

   ◆ Caffeine

   ◆ Alcohol

   ◆ Nicotine

   ◆ Diet

   ◆ Exercise

2. Optimize your surroundings for a good night's sleep, including identifying and making changes to:

   ◆ Noise level

◆ Light

◆ Room temperature

◆ Air quality

◆ Bed comfort

◆ Clothing choices

3. Use the Environment and Sleep Compromise Worksheet to address changes with your bed partner.

Chapter 6

Time to Sleep: Sleep Scheduling

The best quality sleep is restorative and moves repeatedly through all the sleep stages throughout the night. Broken sleep is nonrestorative and leaves you feeling tired the next day. Sleep can be broken for many reasons. Sometimes people fall sleep easily but have trouble staying asleep and awaken after only three or four hours. Others take naps during the day or early evening and sleep a few more hours at night. Many people who have experienced trauma are awakened by nightmares and have difficulty returning to sleep. Sleeping in one block of time is much more recuperative and restful than broken sleep (Morin and Espie 2003). Even if the total number of hours of sleep is the same, getting it all in one consecutive block of time rather than in segments is your goal.

If you have nightmares, before proceeding you may want to use the strategies in chapter 8, where you'll learn ways to cope with and reduce nightmares. Some people can use the sleep scheduling materials better after they've reduced the impact of trauma-related nightmares.

Caution: If you've been diagnosed with bipolar disorder or seizure disorder, please skip the current chapter as the techniques discussed can cause these conditions to worsen (Smith et al. 2003).

In this chapter you will:

♦ Track your total sleep time

♦ Set your morning awake time

♦   Plan your sleep schedule

♦   Learn to consolidate your sleep

♦   *Steven's Story*

Steven experienced a tornado very close to his home. When the tornado came through town, he and his family sought shelter in a closet. He heard the winds howling and the debris flying around outside. Then he heard a sound like a freight train, and he and his family huddled together helplessly as the tornado tore through the area. After the wind and noise died down, Steven and his family cautiously left the closet. To their relief, everything inside their home was alright. Outside, however, they saw that their neighbors' houses had sustained a lot of damage, as had the exterior of their own home.

Ever since the tornado, Steven has slept poorly. Previously, he got about six to seven hours of sleep a night. Since the tornado, he typically gets into bed around 10 p.m. But he doesn't fall asleep until 12 or 12:30 a.m., and he is awake again by 3 a.m. Sometimes, he falls back asleep quickly; other times he is awake for hours. When this happens, he might fall asleep again at about 5 a.m. and stay asleep for one to three hours. No matter how hard he tries to fall or stay asleep, he doesn't feel rested and refreshed in the morning, as he did prior to the tornado.

Let's consider the issues related to Steven's sleep since the tornado:

♦   Before the tornado, Steven slept six to seven hours a night.

♦   Since the tornado, Steven continued getting six to seven total hours of broken sleep most nights.

♦   Even when he sleeps the same number of hours as before the tornado, he doesn't feel rested.

Sleep broken into segments is not as refreshing, restorative, or recuperative as the same number of hours slept in one block of time. Sleep that lasts only a few hours is not deep sleep. Remember, normal sleep cycles through all of the stages of sleep in sequence, several times over the course of one night.

Scheduling and restricting your sleep, or consolidating it into one block of time, is an effective strategy to alleviate insomnia (Spielman, Saskin, and Thorpy 1987; Wohlgemuth and Edinger 2000). It's important to develop a schedule for your sleep. As children we often followed a sleep schedule, and parents usually have one for their children, but as adults we often don't schedule sleep. Your post-trauma sleep disturbance can improve if you begin scheduling your sleep again. Consolidating your sleep into one block of time will help you achieve better quality sleep.

In this chapter we'll explain how to schedule and consolidate your sleep.

TRACK YOUR TOTAL SLEEP TIME

Think about how much total sleep you get on a typical night. If you've already used the Nightly Sleep Tracking Form from chapter 2, you can use it to estimate your total sleep time. If not, use the Total Sleep Time Tracking Worksheet below for the next five days, to determine your average total sleep time. Note that your average amount of sleep time includes napping. The more accurately you estimate your total sleep time, the better you'll be able to schedule your sleep to get a better night's rest.

Total Sleep Time Tracking Worksheet		
Day 1		**Number of Hours Slept**
Daytime nap	_____ a.m/p.m. to _____ a.m/p.m.	
	_____ a.m/p.m. to _____ a.m/p.m.	
	_____ a.m/p.m. to _____ a.m/p.m.	
Nighttime sleep	_____ a.m/p.m. to _____ a.m/p.m.	
	_____ a.m/p.m. to _____ a.m/p.m.	
	_____ a.m/p.m. to _____ a.m/p.m.	
Your Day 1 Total Sleep Time (if less than five hours, write 5)		
Day 2		**Number of Hours Slept**
Daytime nap	_____ a.m/p.m. to _____ a.m/p.m.	
	_____ a.m/p.m. to _____ a.m/p.m.	
	_____ a.m/p.m. to _____ a.m/p.m.	
Nighttime sleep	_____ a.m/p.m. to _____ a.m/p.m.	
	_____ a.m/p.m. to _____ a.m/p.m.	
	_____ a.m/p.m. to _____ a.m/p.m.	
	_____ a.m/p.m. to _____ a.m/p.m.	
Your Day 2 Total Sleep Time (if less than five hours, write 5)		

Day 3		Number of Hours Slept
Daytime nap	_____ a.m/p.m. to _____ a.m/p.m.	
	_____ a.m/p.m. to _____ a.m/p.m.	
	_____ a.m/p.m. to _____ a.m/p.m.	
Nighttime sleep	_____ a.m/p.m. to _____ a.m/p.m.	
	_____ a.m/p.m. to _____ a.m/p.m.	
	_____ a.m/p.m. to _____ a.m/p.m.	
	_____ a.m/p.m. to _____ a.m/p.m.	
Your Day 3 Total Sleep Time (if less than five hours, write 5)		
Day 4		Number of Hours Slept
Daytime nap	_____ a.m/p.m. to _____ a.m/p.m.	
	_____ a.m/p.m. to _____ a.m/p.m.	
	_____ a.m/p.m. to _____ a.m/p.m.	
Nighttime sleep	_____ a.m/p.m. to _____ a.m/p.m.	
	_____ a.m/p.m. to _____ a.m/p.m.	
	_____ a.m/p.m. to _____ a.m/p.m.	
Your Day 4 Total Sleep Time (if less than five hours, write 5)		
Day 5		Number of Hours Slept
Daytime Nap	_____ a.m/p.m. to _____ a.m/p.m.	
	_____ a.m/p.m. to _____ a.m/p.m.	
	_____ a.m/p.m. to _____ a.m/p.m.	
Nighttime Sleep	_____ a.m/p.m. to _____ a.m/p.m.	
	_____ a.m/p.m. to _____ a.m/p.m.	
	_____ a.m/p.m. to _____ a.m/p.m.	
Your Day 5 Total Sleep Time (if less than five hours, write 5)		

CALCULATE YOUR AVERAGE TOTAL SLEEP TIME

Find your Average Total Sleep time by adding up your Total Sleep Time from all five days and then dividing that number by 5:

Your Average Total Sleep Time =

_____ (Day 1 Total Sleep Time)

+

_____ (Day 2 Total Sleep Time)

+

_____ (Day 3 Total Sleep Time)

+

_____ (Day 4 Total Sleep Time)

+

_____ (Day 5 Total Sleep Time)

=

_____ ÷ 5 = _____ (Average Total Sleep Time)

If your Average Total Sleep Time is less than five hours, use 5 hours.

Your Average Total Sleep Time is _____ .

SET YOUR MORNING WAKE-UP TIME

To begin a regular sleep schedule, it's important not to spend more time in bed than your average total sleep time. To do this, decide on a set time that you will rise every morning, and put this into daily practice. A set time for waking up will help you regulate your internal clock and settle into a sleep pattern. You can use an alarm clock to help you rise at the same time every morning.

Your awake time should be the same every morning—no matter how much or how little sleep you got the night before. This develops a consistent sleep-wake cycle. Although you cannot control when you fall asleep or how much you sleep, you can control when you awaken and whether you nap during the day. If you don't allow yourself to oversleep in the morning or to nap during the day, this will begin regulating your sleep-wake cycle and encourage your body to sleep at night.

When deciding on your wake-up time, consider these factors: how much time you need before leaving for work, child care responsibilities, morning appointments, your exercise schedule, and other important morning activities. Set your awake time so you'll have enough time to get ready for your day.

Remember that scheduling your sleep means getting up at the same time every day, seven days a week. You may know people without insomnia who sleep late on weekends, and you might think this a good way to catch up on lost sleep. However, this can backfire and make it harder for you to maintain quality sleep.

Your Morning Awake Time: You will get out of bed at _____ a.m.

PLAN YOUR SLEEP SCHEDULE

It's time to consolidate your sleep and get it all into one time period by planning your sleep schedule. Decide a time to go to bed by subtracting your Average Total Sleep Time from your Morning Awake Time. For example, if you decide to get up by 6 a.m., and your Average Total Sleep Time is five hours of sleep a night, then your in-bed time is 1 a.m. (6 a.m. – 5 hours = 1 a.m.). Don't get into bed before 1 a.m. This is your earliest bedtime.

If your bedtime arrives and you aren't sleepy, don't get into bed until you are sleepy. Continue your bedtime wind-down activities until you're sleepy. The more time you need to wait, the more bedtime wind-down activities you'll need to incorporate into your routine. Getting into bed early to catch up on sleep or getting into bed when you're not sleepy, just because it's bedtime, won't be good strategies for falling asleep quickly, easily, or consistently.

Use the Sleep Schedule Worksheet below to determine when you should schedule your sleep. Use the information you've gathered in this chapter to fill out this worksheet.

Sleep Schedule Worksheet

1. Your Morning Awake Time is _____ a.m.

2. Your Average Total Sleep Time is _____ hours.

3. Find your Morning Awake Time on the chart below and circle it.

4. Start at your circled Morning Awake Time and move backward by your Average Total Sleep Time hours. For example, if your Average Total Sleep Time is five hours of sleep, move back five hours from your circled rising time. Draw a square around this number.

7	8	9	10	11	12	1	2	3	4	5	6	7	8	9
p.m.	p.m.	p.m.	p.m.	p.m.	a.m.	a.m.	a.m.	a.m.	a.m.	a.m.	a.m.	a.m.	a.m.	a.m.

The number with a square around it is your Scheduled Sleep Time. Use this time as your bedtime, but go to bed at this time only if you are sleepy. Remember to use your bedtime wind-down routine and relaxation strategies to become sleepy at this Scheduled Sleep Time.

Your Scheduled Sleep Time: The earliest you will go to bed is _____ p.m./a.m., but only if you're sleepy at that time.

Here's how Steven used the worksheet to determine his sleep schedule.

Steven's Sleep Schedule Worksheet

1. Your Morning Awake Time is *6 a.m.*

2. Your Average Total Sleep time is *6 hours*.

3. Find your Morning Awake Time on the chart below and circle it.

4. Start at your circled Morning Awake Time and move backward by your Average Total Sleep Time hours. Steven's Average Total Sleep Time is six hours, and his Morning Awake Time is 6 a.m. He moved back from 6 a.m. by six hours and drew a square around this number. Steven's Scheduled Sleep Time is 12 a.m. This is the earliest he can get into bed.

7 p.m.	8 p.m.	9 p.m.	10 p.m.	11 p.m.	12 a.m.	1 a.m.	2 a.m.	3 a.m.	4 a.m.	5 a.m.	6 a.m.	7 a.m.	8 a.m.	9 a.m.

Steven's scheduled bedtime is 12 a.m. Therefore, he never gets into bed earlier than 12 a.m., and gets into bed then only if he is sleepy at that time. He pays attention to his signs of sleepiness, such as diminished energy, aching muscles, and yawning. He doesn't go to bed before his 12 a.m. bedtime, even if he is sleepy.

PUT YOUR SLEEP SCHEDULE INTO ACTION

Remember, your goal is to get all of your sleep in one block of time each night, including waking up at the same time every morning. For your sleep plan to work, you must follow it every night, including weekends. You are retraining your body to get restful, restorative sleep; to do this you must adhere to your sleep schedule as much as possible.

Your partner or other people you know may get up at different times each morning or sleep in on weekends. You may have been able to do this at one time yourself. But when your problem is insomnia, your body is telling you that an erratic sleep schedule no longer works for you.

INCREASE THE QUANTITY OF YOUR SLEEP

When you've implemented your sleep schedule and seen that your broken sleep has consolidated, then you can add to the amount of time you sleep. How do you know if your sleep is consolidated? Calculate your total sleep time each night and compare it to the total amount of time you spend in bed. This is known as *sleep efficiency*. When your total sleep time is at least 90 percent of the total amount of time you spend in bed (meaning that at least 90 percent of your time in bed is spent sleeping), you can gradually add to your time in bed (Morin and Espie 2003).

Calculate Your Sleep Efficiency:

Total Sleep Time _____ ÷ Time in Bed _____ = _____ .

Your Sleep Efficiency is your Total Sleep Time divided by your Time in Bed.

Let's see how Steven is sleeping. After following his sleep schedule for about two weeks, he decided to calculate his sleep efficiency. Steven observed that he was getting about 5.5 total hours of sleep a night. Some nights he got even more sleep, and he noticed that he started feeling sleepier earlier than his bedtime. He was waking up at 6 a.m., in accord with his sleep schedule, and he was getting into bed at midnight.

Steven's Sleep Efficiency:

My total Time in Bed is 6 hours.

My Total Sleep Time is 5.5 hours.

My Sleep Efficiency is 5.5 hours ÷ 6 hours = .92 or 92 percent

Steven has successfully become accustomed to his new sleep schedule. He knows this because his sleep efficiency is greater than 90 percent.

When you become accustomed to your new sleep schedule, you can add fifteen minutes to your sleep by getting into bed fifteen minutes earlier. Try this for one week. If your body becomes successfully accustomed to this new bedtime (at least 90 percent sleep efficiency), add another fifteen minutes the following week. Use the worksheet below to increase your sleep time minutes.

Increasing Your Sleep Time Worksheet

Directions: Move your bedtime fifteen minutes earlier for one week. Discontinue if your amount of sleep decreases or stops increasing.

	Scheduled Sleep Time	Morning Awake time*	Hours of Sleep	Sleep Efficiency Rating (hours asleep ÷ hours in bed = sleep efficiency rating)
Week 1				____ ÷ ____ = ____
Week 2				____ ÷ ____ = ____
Week 3				____ ÷ ____ = ____
Week 4				____ ÷ ____ = ____
Week 5				____ ÷ ____ = ____
Week 6				____ ÷ ____ = ____

* Morning Awake Time is the time you get out of bed, regardless of how you've slept. You can get up earlier, but not later.

In Steven's example below, he went to bed at 12 a.m. and usually got 5.5 hours of sleep before getting up at 6 a.m. His sleep efficiency indicated he could increase his sleep time by going to bed fifteen minutes earlier.

So, for the first week he charted his sleep efficiency, it was 92 percent. During week 2, he began getting into bed at 11:45 p.m., and because his sleep efficiency was still high after that week (92 percent), he started getting into bed at 11:30 p.m. the third week. However, because his sleep efficiency dropped to 88 percent, he resumed his bedtime of 11:45 p.m. After again reaching 92 percent sleep efficiency, Steven tried to add fifteen more minutes to his sleep time; however, because this didn't result in 90 percent or greater sleep efficiency, he changed his bedtime back to 11:45 p.m.

The key for Steven was to monitor his ability to initiate sleep earlier and to stop when he was unable to sleep at least 90 percent of the time between his bedtime and awake time. Let's look at his worksheet.

Steven's Increasing Your Sleep Time Worksheet

Directions: Move your bedtime fifteen minutes earlier for one week. Discontinue if your amount of sleep decreases or stops increasing.

	Scheduled Sleep Time	Morning Awake Time*	Hours of Sleep	Sleep Efficiency Rating (hours asleep ÷ hours in bed = sleep efficiency rating)
Week 1	12:00 a.m.	6 a.m.	5 hours, 30 minutes	5.5 ÷ 6= 92%
Week 2	11:45 p.m.	6 a.m.	5 hours, 45 min.	5.5 ÷ 6.25 = 92%
Week 3	11:30 p.m.	6 a.m.	5 hours, 45 min.	5.75 ÷ 6.5 = 88%
Week 4	11:45 p.m.	6 a.m.	5 hours, 45 min.	5.75 ÷ 6.25 = 92%
Week 5	11:30 p.m.	6 a.m.	5 hours, 45 minutes	5.75 ÷ 6.5 = 88%
Week 6	11:45 p.m.	6 a.m.	5 hours, 45 min.	5.75 ÷ 6.25 = 92%

* Morning Awake Time is the time you get out of bed, regardless of how you've slept. You can get up earlier, but not later.

Notice that Steven began moving his bedtime earlier only after he was able to get 90 percent sleep efficiency between his bedtime and awake time. He was unable to achieve 90 percent efficiency when he was in bed for more than six and a quarter hours (weeks 3 and 5). Therefore, he set his bedtime at 11:45 p.m.

Here is another way to determine whether you're getting 90 percent consolidated sleep. You'll need to multiply the number of hours you allot for sleep (the number of hours between your bedtime and awake time) by 0.90. This is the number of hours of sleep you need to achieve between your bedtime and awake time before moving your bedtime fifteen minutes earlier.

For example, Steven's bedtime of 12 a.m. and awake time of 6 a.m. allots six hours for sleep. He could begin going to bed fifteen minutes earlier when he achieves 5.4 (roughly five and a half) hours of sleep (6 hours x 0.90 = 5.4).

Try building on your success by moving your bedtime fifteen minutes earlier after your sleep has become consolidated. Add fifteen minutes to your sleep time each week until the amount of time you sleep stops increasing.

UTILIZING SUPPORT

Creating a new sleep schedule that requires you to alter the time you go to bed at night and the time you awaken in the morning can affect your significant other. Again, it's important to educate your partner so he or she will understand how this treatment will help you and be mutually beneficial. Having support for this treatment can help you achieve success. Discuss your new sleep schedule with your partner before implementing any changes. If your significant other is your bed partner, setting an alarm to awaken you every morning may awaken your partner too.

Try to find a mutually agreeable time for rising in the morning. Or try placing your alarm clock on your side of the bed to lessen the chance that your partner will be awakened at an unwanted hour.

Your partner may want to sleep in on weekends, while you need to adhere to your sleep schedule every day. Do everything you can to avoid waking your partner at a time when he or she doesn't want to get up. Wear socks or quiet slippers rather than noisy shoes. Leave the bedroom as quietly and quickly as possible to decrease the chance that you will awaken your partner.

Similarly, when you're waiting to go to bed at night, it's likely that your bedtime will be later than your partner's. While you're waiting for your bedtime, engage in quiet, relaxing, and soothing activities that won't disrupt your partner's sleep. When entering your room at bedtime, do so as quietly as possible and avoid turning on any lights.

Talk to your partner about how important this part of your treatment is. Indeed, sleep consolidation is one of the single most effective behavioral therapies for insomnia.

OVERCOMING OBSTACLES AND PLANNING FOR SUCCESS

It's common for people to encounter some difficulties when making a sleep schedule. When you are sleep-deprived, it can be hard knowing that you must follow a strict sleep schedule. Your sleep schedule may mean you'll get less sleep for a short time until your body adjusts to your new schedule. As a result, you may feel more fatigued during the day.

Remind yourself that although scheduling your sleep may lead initially to less sleep, you'll soon see results in the increased quantity and quality of your sleep. Remember, this is a highly effective strategy for overcoming insomnia and improving sleep quality. Be persistent and know that better sleep is within your reach.

SUGGESTED GOAL ASSIGNMENT

Now you've learned to plan your sleep. Continue building on your success.

1. Understand your sleep better by using the Total Sleep Time Tracking Worksheet.

2. Set a morning awake time.

3. Determine your scheduled sleep time.

4. Practice your sleep schedule nightly.

Chapter 7

Sleep Beliefs: How You Think Affects How You Sleep

You may have misconceptions about your sleep for several reasons. It is very difficult to judge your own sleep because the behavior you want to evaluate occurs when you are, well, asleep. Also, many myths and misunderstandings about sleep exist. Everyone knows that people need eight hours of sleep to function well the next day, right?

Because you suffer from insomnia, you've probably developed some habits of thought about sleep that keep you from getting a good night's rest. In this chapter, you'll learn to recognize and examine your thoughts and beliefs about sleep and work toward a more balanced, accurate view of your sleep.

The goals of this chapter are:

◆ To be more objective about your sleep

◆ To identify myths about sleep

◆ To identify and challenge your sleep-related thoughts and beliefs

◆ To learn journaling to cope with thoughts and stressors that interfere with sleep

◆ To learn to tolerate and be less distressed by worries about sleep

OBSERVING YOUR SLEEP

Research and clinical experience have shown that people tend to underestimate the amount of time they slept the night before and overestimate the time needed to fall asleep (Harvey, Tang, and Browning 2005). We know this because what people report about their sleep can be compared to objective data derived from a sleep study (or polysomnography).

You may have had a sleep study and have some awareness of your objective sleep status. Even if you haven't, it is important to understand that you might be sleeping better than you think. Although not as accurate as a sleep study, a sleep diary (like the Nightly Sleep Tracking Form in chapter 2) can help you observe your sleep more accurately than you can by thinking about it. If you haven't already done so, use the Nightly Sleep Tracking Form to monitor your sleep for one week. Then compare your findings to your initial beliefs about your sleep, which you'll explore in a moment. Do your findings reveal you sleep more or less than you thought you did? Besides being a poor judge of your own objective sleep status, it's likely that you overestimate the importance of sleep and the impact of insomnia on your daytime functioning.

Most people with insomnia do get enough sleep to function, but they spend a lot of time worrying about the consequences of poor sleep. Let's look at how people make judgments about their sleep and its impact on their functioning. Consider Sara, who experienced insomnia as a young adult.

◆ *Sara's Story*

Sara was molested by her father when she was a teenager. The abuse often occurred at night in her bedroom. Sara has talked to a therapist about her traumatic experiences, and she has worked through many of her fears and other post-trauma reactions. Now, years later, Sara believes that she has recovered from the abuse in most ways. She lives alone and has a long-term boyfriend and many close friends. She loves her job and excels at it.

In spite of doing well in most areas of her life, Sara continues having frequent bouts of insomnia, which she finds quite distressing. She believes she doesn't sleep well most nights and that her sleep is much worse than most people's. As bedtime approaches, she becomes increasingly

anxious about what the night will be like. She awakens in the night to sounds that remind her of the molestation. Sometimes she thinks an intruder has entered her bedroom. When this occurs, she feels terrified. Her heart pounds and her mind races as she prepares for danger. This high level of physiological arousal awakens her even further and results in frustration, anxiety, and anger. As a result, her chances of returning to sleep diminish. After such a night, Sara feels angry and frustrated. She thinks something must be wrong with her and tells herself she'll never be normal. She worries about how she will function at work the next day, because she believes that without sleep, she isn't as good at her job as she is after a good night's sleep. She worries she'll be fired because of her poor performance. She wonders whether to call in sick the next day, thinking it's better to stay home than work and do a poor job. Sara worries about how she looks the day after a sleepless night. She believes that others can tell when she hasn't had a good night's sleep. She worries about what people think about her and believes they'll know something is wrong with her.

Here are the important points about Sara's story:

◆ Sara believes her sleep is more disrupted than most people's.

◆ She believes her poor sleep indicates she is abnormal and that something is wrong with her.

◆ Sara excels at her job and has healthy relationships.

◆ She worries about her ability to sleep. These worries make it harder for her to return to sleep once she's awakened.

◆ Sara worries about the effects of insomnia on her work performance and personal relationships. These worries make her feel more anxious as bedtime approaches because so much depends on her getting a good night's sleep.

If Sara were to monitor her sleep for one or two weeks, she might be surprised to discover that she sleeps more than she thinks she does. Moreover, she might benefit from examining her thoughts and beliefs about her sleep. Most people sleep poorly sometimes. Giving too much importance to sleep problems doesn't take into account how well we can function even with a poor night's sleep. Sara has evidence that she functions well (a good job, healthy relationships) in spite of her poor sleep, but she ignores or minimizes the evidence to focus on the real or anticipated negative consequences of insomnia. Finally, she finds it difficult to manage and recuperate from trauma-related intrusive thoughts at night.

SLEEP MYTHS AND MISCONCEPTIONS

We learn many myths and misconceptions about sleep from parents, friends, and our culture. Check off all of your beliefs about sleep and your sleep problems:

_____ Everyone needs at least eight hours of sleep at night.

__✓__ When people can't sleep well, that means something is really wrong.

_____ Normal people sleep well every night.

__✓__ When people can't sleep at night, it causes irritability the next day.

__✓__ Sleep problems lead to depression and anxiety.

__✓__ Insomnia makes it hard for people to get things done the next day.

_____ If people try hard enough, they can make themselves sleep.

_____ After a poor night's sleep, people are less productive.

_____ There is nothing I can do to sleep better.

_____ I will never get a good night's sleep.

How many items did you check off? None of these statements is absolutely true. All represent common misconceptions about sleep that actually may contribute to your insomnia. When you hold yourself to unrealistic standards, you won't meet these standards. Even if some of these statements are true for you now or were true in your past, it's important to understand that your sleep won't respond well to worry, fear, or anxiety. Fears and worries just make sleep harder to come by.

If you hold beliefs about sleep based on myths or misconceptions, you unwittingly may worsen or contribute to your insomnia. You may have some of these thoughts during the day when you're awake, and at night while lying in bed. It's important to identify the beliefs, thoughts, and images you have about your inability to sleep well.

Identifying and understanding your thoughts will allow you to determine their effect on your sleep and, more importantly, allow you to change them. For example, Sara believes her sleep is more disrupted than others'. She thinks her poor sleep negatively impacts her work, and she worries about losing her job.

Use the following Sleep Cognitions Tracking Worksheet to monitor your thoughts and beliefs about sleep.

Sleep Cognitions Tracking Worksheet

Situation	Feelings	Images, Thoughts, or Beliefs
Middle of night; can't sleep		
Morning after a night of poor sleep		
Daytime after a night of poor sleep		

Sara recognized that worrying about sleep might interfere with her ability to rest at night. She used the Sleep Cognitions Tracking Worksheet to track her thoughts about her insomnia. Let's look at Sara's completed form.

Sara's Sleep Cognitions Tracking Worksheet		
Situation	**Feelings**	**Images, Thoughts, or Beliefs**
Middle of night; can't sleep	*Anxious, bad* *Ashamed*	*There must be something really wrong with me.* *I'm ashamed of the molestation.*
Morning after a night of poor sleep	*Distressed, upset* *Worried, fearful*	*My sleep is much worse than anyone else's. I will never get a good night's sleep.* *I'm not able to go to work. I might lose my job.*
Daytime after a night of poor sleep	*Worried, nervous* *Incompetent, like a failure*	*People will notice I don't look or act rested.* *I can't go to a meeting and be effective. I can see myself looking exhausted and being unable to handle my job.*

EXAMINE YOUR THOUGHTS AND BELIEFS ABOUT SLEEP

Let's examine some myths and misconceptions from the checklist. Since it's unlikely that you can be objective about your sleep, prepare to test your beliefs and recognize that there may be alternative information to consider. To test and challenge your beliefs and consider new information, it's important to keep an open mind. See chapter 1 for objective information about normal sleep and the effects of insomnia. We will review some of that information here.

After a traumatic event, beliefs about sleep can cause, worsen, and maintain insomnia. Examining your thoughts and beliefs about sleep ensures that you take into account all of the available information and evidence. Then you'll have a more balanced perspective on your sleep—one that will promote rather than impede a good night's rest.

How Beliefs About Sleep Add to Sleep Problems

In his book *Insomnia: A Clinical Guide to Assessment and Treatment* (Morin and Espie 2003), sleep specialist Charles Morin discusses the importance of changing certain beliefs and attitudes about sleep as an essential component of cognitive behavioral therapy (CBT) for insomnia. Let's examine some common beliefs about insomnia that are neither balanced nor accurate. These kinds of unhelpful thoughts lead to bad feelings and must be challenged. Consider those that apply to you. How can you challenge your imprecise thinking using the information provided here and in chapter 1?

- ◆ If I were normal, I would be able to sleep. Something is terribly wrong with me. I'll never get a good night's sleep.

Why do you think you have trouble sleeping? Do normal people sometimes sleep poorly? What does it mean that you can't sleep? Are there things you can do to improve your sleep? Worrying about sleep can disrupt it, so it's important to be well educated about insomnia. Remember, many factors can impact how well you sleep. People who haven't experienced trauma can also have difficulty sleeping, for a variety of reasons. Just because you didn't sleep well last night and the night before doesn't mean you won't sleep well ever again. Examine your thoughts and beliefs about sleep to be sure you aren't causing yourself unnecessary stress. Reread chapter 1 on why sleep problems develop after a trauma, to see if your thoughts about your sleep problems are accurate and balanced.

- ◆ I should be getting eight hours of sleep at night.

Keep your expectations realistic. Not everyone needs eight hours of sleep. There are individual differences in sleep needs. Also, sleep need varies across life span. As you age, you sleep less. Review your Nightly Sleep Tracking Form (see chapter 2) to determine how much sleep you need to feel rested. Look for variations in your sleep pattern over time. Some nights you may sleep better than others. Examine your ratings of how refreshing your sleep was each night you monitored it, and use these ratings to determine how many hours you slept when you felt most refreshed. The key is to get the best quality sleep possible at this time in your life. Review chapter 1 for information on variations in the normal sleep pattern.

- ◆ I can't get things done during the day because I'm so tired.

Worrying about sleep problems can increase sleep difficulties. What evidence do you have from your experience that you can function even on very little sleep? Be objective. Try an experiment on yourself: What are you afraid you won't accomplish the day after you've slept poorly? Use the Task Chart below to test your concerns. Use this chart over a five-day period, even if they're not five consecutive days. Choose days when you believe you didn't sleep well the night before, and write down the tasks you'd planned to accomplish that day. Then note whether you accomplished them, how successful you were, and how you felt afterward.

Task Chart

	Task	Attempted to Accomplish	% Successful (0-100)	Feelings Afterward
10/10	Clean out - carpet furnace room	Accomplished	100%	Good - positive
10/11	Full yard work	Accompl.	90%	Relieved
10/12	Basement work	Accomp.	80°	Good
10/13	Assign with 5h - Run	Yes	100%	Surprised Relieved
10/15	House photos	Yes	90°	Glad

Sara's Task Chart

Task	Attempted to Accomplish	% Successful (0-100)	Feelings Afterward
Lead book club discussion	No	0%	Disappointed
Meet with supervisor to go over new project	Yes	70%	Relieved, happy
Go for walk with friend	No	0%	Lonely, frustrated
Have romantic birthday dinner with boyfriend	Yes	60%	Satisfied, proud

In Sara's example, she decided she was too tired to lead her book club discussion because of poor sleep, even though she'd committed to this some time ago. She backed out at the last minute and, as a result, felt disappointed. She rated her success at accomplishing this activity as 0 percent. Another time, she decided to meet her boss to go over an important project even though she felt tired because of sleeping badly the previous night. She rated her success at this task at 70 percent, not as high as she might have if she'd been fully rested, but mostly successful. She felt happy and relieved to have had the meeting. Her Task Chart shows that Sara feels better when she does activities in spite of her insomnia than when she avoids them.

It's likely that not trying to do important activities leaves you disappointed and perhaps even more stressed about your sleep problems. Not attempting what you want to accomplish ensures a 0 percent success rate and adds more fuel to the "insomnia worry" fire. Worrying about insomnia or avoiding activities because of fatigue does nothing to solve sleep problems or help you accomplish more during the day.

Instead, worry and avoidance just add to sleep problems, giving nighttime anxiety and dread and daytime worry even more power. If you try to reach your goals even when fatigued, you're likely to have a success rate higher than 0 and take back your life from insomnia. Furthermore, the more activities you participate in during the day, the likelier it is that you'll sleep well at night.

Don't let insomnia get the best of you! After a poor night's sleep, it's best to go on with planned activities as much as possible and minimize the disruption insomnia has in your life. Don't allow sleep problems to become more important than daytime priorities. Trust your body and remember that even with insomnia, your body allows you to get enough sleep to function (see chapter 1). Don't change your activities based on lack of sleep, but strive instead to perform your daytime activities no matter what your sleep was like the night before. After a poor night's rest you may feel tired, but notice that you can still proceed with important activities. During the day, when you do something important or pleasurable, this will help to disconfirm your belief that a good night's sleep is essential (Morin and Espie 2003). Engaging in activity in spite of insomnia helps to break the insomnia cycle.

- I'm irritable during the day because I can't sleep at night. I wouldn't be depressed or anxious if I could sleep at night.

Be careful not to attribute all of your problems to insomnia. You may notice that your depression and irritability or other mood symptoms lessen with improved sleep. However, your insomnia is not necessarily or 100 percent responsible for your daytime mood. It's likely that your mood isn't stable but varies throughout the day. When you are in a poor mood, it's important to try to cope with it. The strategies you learn here will help with your sleep. Use other coping skills or treatment workbooks to learn to control irritability, anxiety, or depression. You may have to address these problems separately from sleep issues. In other words, there are many reasons trauma survivors may feel depressed, irritable, and anxious, aside from not getting enough sleep. If you are distressed by mood disturbances, it's important to explore your situation and perhaps talk to a mental health professional.

- If I try hard, I can force myself to sleep.

Sleep is an activity we cannot force. Trying to force sleep requires effort, engages and alerts the brain, and is not relaxing, all of which work against sleep. Exerting effort at bedtime is contrary to relaxing and letting go, which is the best way to ensure good sleep. Practice this workbook's strategies over time, and have confidence in their ability to help you improve your sleep.

 ◆ I get overwhelmed by fear at night.

Trauma survivors often perceive nighttime as dangerous. For Sara, lying in bed at night hearing strange sounds triggers memories of her molestation, along with fears for her safety. Perhaps you also feel that you must be on guard for danger at night. This may stem from your traumatic experience, especially if it occurred at night. Learn to recognize when your nighttime behaviors and beliefs are based on past trauma rather than present reality. Catch yourself when your trauma is "talking." Pay attention to signs of safety at night rather than signs of danger. Say to yourself, "My house alarm is set" or "The noises I hear outside pass with no resulting danger." Use these statements to focus on the present reality rather than letting your past take over. Use the insomnia coping statements and other strategies in the section Challenging Thoughts About Insomnia, later in this chapter, to increase your tolerance for anxiety.

JOURNALING

Much like worries about daily tasks, events, and other life stressors, thoughts and worries about sleep interfere with your ability to rest. When you're having a hard time managing stress at work or at home, your sleep can be disrupted. Similarly, when you're faced with the stress of insomnia, your worries about it and its consequences can add to your sleep disruption. It's important to address daily stressors and learn to challenge and change your beliefs about sleep in a way that facilitates being less anxious and more relaxed throughout the day and at night. Journaling is a technique that has proved helpful in reducing stress (Murray 2002).

Everyday stressors and stress related to insomnia can affect your sleep, perhaps even more than they did before your trauma. To cope with worries, concerns, and emotions related to insomnia and other stresses in your life, you'll learn a journaling technique that will alleviate some of the stress that may be impeding you from falling asleep faster, and help you identify your beliefs, thoughts, and worries about insomnia.

The Benefits of Journaling

Journaling is a way to write about one's life that promotes insight and relief. Journaling differs from simply writing, as it has specific parameters that promote the relief of emotional tension and the development of awareness and insight. Research has shown that people who do journaling or write to heal (Pennebaker 1997) are healthier physically and mentally (Pennebaker, Kiecolt-Glaser, and Glaser 1988).

How Journaling Can Help You Sleep Better

For individuals struggling with insomnia, thoughts and worries before bedtime are a major impediment to their ability to fall asleep (Harvey 2000). These thoughts and worries may include beliefs about sleeplessness and the impact of insomnia on their lives. Worries about other life issues (such as work, money, or family concerns) also can prevent sleep onset (Wicklow and Espie 2000). Research has shown that journaling about your problems results in increased ability to fall asleep quickly (Harvey and Farrell 2003). Therefore, to improve your ability to fall asleep, we suggest journaling for stress relief. Note that it's important to do your journaling before you do your bedtime wind-down routine.

How to Use Your Journal for Stress Relief

Journaling for stress relief differs from keeping a diary. With journaling, you don't write daily for an extended period of time. Also, you don't write about everyday, routine events; instead, you focus on topics that have meaning for you. Unlike other types of writing, journaling doesn't necessarily involve writing in complete sentences, editing, or sharing with others. Journaling is only for you.

EXERCISE: Writing in Your Journal

The following instructions were adapted from Pennebaker 2004, with permission from New Harbinger Publications.

1. Choose a quiet place to journal where you can concentrate and won't be interrupted. If possible, choose a different place than where you usually work.

2. Write about something meaningful to you or something that's bothering you. Choose something you are dealing with now, rather than something from your past. Be sure to include your thoughts and feelings, both positive and negative, in your writing.

3. Write about your insomnia. Include all of your thoughts about your sleep problems. What goes through your mind about your sleep? What does having insomnia mean about you? What is your worst fear about insomnia and how it affects you?

4. Write continuously for at least twenty minutes each journaling session. You may want to leave yourself some time afterward, to process the thoughts and emotions that came up while journaling.

5. Write every day for four consecutive days. You can write about the same thing every day, or different issues each session. If you start writing about one thing and find yourself writing about another, it's okay to follow your thoughts, as long as your writing continues to have meaning for you. If you get bored with writing or your mind wanders, redirect your writing to something that has meaning for you.

6. Don't stop to read or judge what you write. Editing your writing might interfere with the process. Remember this writing is only for you. You may hide it or dispose of it once you have finished. Don't write something with the purpose of sharing it (a letter, for example). If you want to share what you write, rewrite it later in a different form.

7. Although most people prefer to use a pen to write because it is slower and allows more time to think, you may use a computer if that's more comfortable. However, using a computer makes it easier to edit for spelling and grammar—remember not to do this while journaling.

8. If you think you aren't ready to write about something, then don't. If you find yourself writing about something that is too difficult for you emotionally or too overwhelming, stop and write about something else.

Using a notebook or loose-leaf binder, follow the instructions above for four consecutive days.

Note: We aren't advocating that you write about your trauma, but rather about your insomnia, everyday stressors, and emotionally meaningful events that may affect your sleep. If you want to write about or work through your trauma, there are other therapies you can utilize; see the resources section for a list of websites to find a therapist.

REVIEW YOUR JOURNAL

After journaling, you may feel sad or emotionally drained. This is normal and will be short-lived. It may be helpful to review what you've written. This can be done at any point after you've completed the journaling task.

Look over your journaling and circle any statements related to your sleep. These statements might include feelings (for example, frustration, anger, upset, nervousness) related to your insomnia. They might be thoughts about why you have sleep problems or what this means about you. They can include worries about how your insomnia will affect you or the impact it has had on you so far.

As you examine the sleep beliefs in your journal, consider the myths and misconceptions about sleep discussed earlier in this chapter and see whether your beliefs are based on any of these. Can you find any evidence to counter your negative thoughts? Examine your own experience or apply what you know about sleep now. Can you make your thoughts more balanced? Remember, distorted sleep beliefs are based on ideals or myths that don't necessarily apply to you. They might be extreme, all-or-nothing statements that use words like "always" or "never" (for example, "I'll never be able to sleep" or "I'm always tired"). They might be predictions about the future (for example, "If I can't sleep tonight, I'll be no good tomorrow"). By identifying your distorted thoughts and beliefs, you can challenge and change them to be more balanced and accurate. Having more balanced, realistic sleep beliefs will help you feel less anxious, worried, and frustrated. Feeling more relaxed and less worried about your sleep will help improve your sleep.

CHALLENGING THOUGHTS ABOUT INSOMNIA

The idea of challenging your thoughts and beliefs derives from cognitive therapy, pioneered by Aaron Beck and his colleagues (1979). The basis of cognitive therapy is that you are the agent of your emotions. That is, your emotions result from how you think about or interpret situations.

For example, compare Sara's sleep beliefs to those of her friend Emily. Both slept four hours the previous night, so their situations are similar, but their view of their situations differs.

Sara's and Emily's Sleep Beliefs Compared				
	Situation	**Thoughts/Interpretation**	**Resulting Emotion or Mood**	**Behavior**
Sara	*4 hours of sleep*	*This is awful. I can't stand it. I'm going to be exhausted. I'll never be normal. I dread another night like this.*	*Frustrated Depressed Worried*	*Call in sick to work; lie around the house all day.*
Emily	*4 hours of sleep*	*I just need to go about my day. I wish I could get more sleep, but I know I can work even with just 4 hours of sleep. Tonight will be better.*	*Disappointed Resolute Proud Hopeful*	*Go to work and accomplish most tasks planned for the day.*

Sara's thoughts and resulting emotions get the best of her—and her sleep. Her interpretations or sleep beliefs likely worsen and contribute to her sleep problems. Her sleep beliefs lead her to feel depressed and worried, with the result that she doesn't go to work. She spends the day lying around the house, which, in turn, makes it harder for her to get to sleep that night.

Emily's sleep beliefs, on the other hand, don't worsen her sleep or her mood the next day. In fact, her interpretation of her sleeplessness may help her sleep better the next night. Although she's disappointed, she's also determined to work in spite of her sleep problems. She remembers similar times in the past when she went to work and accomplished things even after a poor night's sleep. She's proud of her abilities to persevere in spite of sleep problems, and goes to work and accomplishes her goals for the day. She feels hopeful that she'll sleep better tonight.

Mood and thoughts are linked in such a way that when you examine your mood, you also examine your thoughts. It just takes practice to get into the habit of noticing them. Once you are aware of your thoughts and interpretations, you can learn to change them!

To begin to change your emotions so they don't get the best of you, use coping statements. A list of balanced insomnia coping statements follows:

Insomnia Coping Statements

- I don't like my insomnia, but I can deal with it.

- I won't let my sleep problems interfere with my relationships.

- I can overcome my sleepiness and still do well at work.

- This is tough, but I can handle it.

- I can be in a good mood, even if I didn't sleep well.

- I'm getting enough sleep to function.

- I'm going to have good and bad days.

- Having a bad night's sleep doesn't mean I can't have a good day today.

- People need different amounts of sleep. Many people don't sleep well sometimes.

- I've been able to do my job most days over the last year.

- Just because I didn't sleep well last night doesn't mean I won't sleep well tonight.

Using the table below, identify your distorted thoughts or sleep beliefs in the first column. Try to identify your thoughts by yourself; if you cannot, use the myths about sleep outlined earlier in this chapter to help you identify your unhelpful beliefs. Then identify how the distorted thoughts make you feel (emotions or mood) in the second column. Next, use the relevant insomnia coping statements above (or write your own) to refute these thoughts. Finally, after using the coping statements, see whether you feel differently about your sleep difficulties. Then write down any new emotions or mood changes in the last column.

Distorted Thoughts and Beliefs About Sleep Worksheet

My Sleep Beliefs or Distorted Thoughts about Insomnia	Resulting Emotion or Mood	Insomnia Coping Statement	New Emotion or Mood
I will not accomplish my daily goals with poor sleep	DEPRESSED / PUT OFF	Tough, but can also handle it	RELIEF in control
POOR SLEEP EQUALS A WASTED DAY	~~scribbled out~~ loss	Getting enough sleep to function	RELIEF CALM
I will will make poor decisions with little sleep	~~scribbled~~ in decisive	I can overcome poor sleep	CONFIDENT
POOR SLEEP = NO ENERGY	DEPRESSED DISAPPOINTED	Past experience says I can overcome	RELIEF
POOR SLEEP = POOR WORKOUTS	ANGRY	Past experience shows I can overcome with exercise	good — confident

Here is Sara's example.

Sara's Distorted Thoughts and Beliefs About Sleep Worksheet			
My Sleep Beliefs or Distorted Thoughts about Insomnia	**Resulting Emotion or Mood**	**Insomnia Coping Statement**	**New Emotion or Mood**
There must be something really wrong with me that I can't sleep again tonight.	*Worried Distressed*	*Most people don't sleep well sometimes.*	*Less worried Relieved*
My sleep is much worse than anyone else's. I'll never be able to get a good night's sleep.	*Distressed Hopeless*	*I'm going to have good and bad days.* *Just because I didn't sleep well last night doesn't mean I won't sleep well tonight.*	*Hopeful Calm*
I'm not going to be able to work. I might lose my job.	*Worried Fearful*	*I've been able to do my job most days over the last year.* *I can overcome my sleepiness and still do well at work.* *Having a bad night's sleep doesn't mean I can't have a good day today.*	*Competent Confident Hopeful*

INCREASE YOUR ANXIETY TOLERANCE

Many people who experience a psychological trauma notice their anxiety increases as a result. Anxiety may be related to specific triggers of the trauma (for example, when Sara hears a noise while in bed, it reminds her of her trauma), or it can arise seemingly out of the blue. Acceptance and commitment therapy (ACT) provides some useful strategies for managing anxiety (Hayes, Strosahl, and Wilson 1999). One premise of ACT, based on mindfulness, involves observing and detaching yourself, in a healthy way, from your thoughts rather than being pulled in or consumed by them. Naming thoughts and worries as just that, rather than seeing them as reality, can help to decrease the negative emotions associated with them.

For example, Sara found herself thinking, "I'm afraid that someone is coming into my house to attack me." ACT teaches that Sara can observe this thought and be less impacted by anxiety if she says instead, "I'm having the thought that someone is coming into my house to attack me." The difference is that Sara can now observe her thought as simply that, a thought, and not a reality. Similarly, instead of saying, "I won't be able to work tomorrow if I don't get some sleep tonight," say, "I'm having the worry that I won't be able to work tomorrow if I don't get some sleep tonight."

This technique of labeling your thoughts is a method of what ACT calls cognitive defusion (Hayes 2005). Defusing or separating yourself from your thoughts allows you to gain distance from or perspective on them and reduces their emotional and behavioral impact. For example, consider the difference between the following two statements:

- ◆ I'm a nervous wreck!

- ◆ I'm having the feeling that I'm a nervous wreck.

The first statement sounds like a statement of fact. It gives you no perspective; rather, it tells you what you are: a nervous wreck. It makes it hard not to buy into the idea of being a nervous wreck. In the second statement, you are commenting on how you feel instead of making a factual statement. It leaves open the possibility that this is just a feeling and not necessarily a fact.

EXERCISE: Observe Your Thoughts and Experiences and Label Them

Now try this exercise, adapted from Hayes and Smith 2005, with permission from New Harbinger Publications. For the next five minutes, observe your thoughts, feelings, mental images, and bodily sensations, and then label them. For example, if you're fatigued, note it by saying, "I'm having the bodily sensation of fatigue." If you're feeling angry, label this feeling by saying, "I'm having the feeling of anger."

Use this guide to help you with labeling:

◆ I'm having the thought that… (describe your thought).

◆ I'm having the feeling of… (describe your feeling).

◆ I'm having the image of… (describe the image).

◆ I'm feeling the bodily sensation of… (describe the bodily sensation).

◆ I'm having the urge to… (describe your urge).

Use the space below to practice observing your thoughts and experiences, labeling them as they occur.

I feel I want to accomplish something

I feel I am getting behind

my mind feels tired / stressed

I feel behind in all with

I like the peace - no noise

Cognitive defusion helps you see that you don't have to buy into your thoughts. Thoughts and beliefs aren't necessarily facts. In other words, evaluate your thoughts rather than assuming they are facts. Humans have very active minds. Our minds produce both rational and irrational thoughts, and these thoughts are never-ending. By labeling and observing your thoughts, worries, and anxieties, you stop yourself from being pulled in and decrease your distress as a result.

Increasing your mindfulness also can help you manage your anxiety. Most of your fears and anxieties are about what happened in the past or what might happen in the future, not about what is happening right now at this moment. If you learn to increase your mindfulness skills, or your connection with the present, you can decrease your anxieties and fears. Although you cannot choose what comes into your mind, you can choose what you pay attention to.

EXERCISE: Mindfulness Exercise

Try this mindfulness exercise. Read it through several times and try it for five or ten minutes at a time, going longer each time and gradually increasing your practice. See *Get Out of Your Mind and Into Your Life* (Hayes 2005) for more exercises to increase mindfulness.

Sit upright in a chair and close your eyes or focus on a point on the floor in front of you. Place both feet on the ground and notice the floor under your feet. Notice the chair as it supports your body. Place your hands in your lap in an open, relaxed position. Now focus your attention on some aspect of your breathing. You don't need to change your breathing, just notice it. You can choose how to focus on your breathing. You may choose to focus on your nostrils and notice the feeling of air as it enters and leaves your nose. You may focus on your breath going into your lungs, feeling it go to the bottom of your lungs as you inhale, and feeling it leave your lungs as you exhale. Or you may choose to count your breaths, counting on the out-breath from 1 to 10 and starting over again at 1. As you focus on your breath, notice your mind producing many thoughts. You might notice images, hear sounds, or notice bodily sensations. As your mind wanders to these things, notice the thought, image, or sensation and then gently return to your breathing. You might even notice that you become distracted by your thoughts, and before you know it, you are thinking about a situation from your past or solving a problem related to the future. You might find yourself involved in a train of thought and realize you are no longer focusing on your breathing. As soon as you notice this, simply return to focusing on your breathing. Do this as many times as necessary. Now imagine your thoughts are like leaves floating on a stream. As a thought comes into your mind, neither pull it toward you nor push it away. Instead, watch it pass by and float away like a leaf in a stream.

UTILIZING SUPPORT

Because you cannot be objective about your sleep, it can be very helpful to solicit your partner's opinions about how your lack of sleep affects you. You can ask your partner or someone close to you if he or she has observed any change in your behavior or mood after you failed to get a good night's rest. You can ask how your insomnia affects this person and your relationship with him or her. This can be a difficult conversation, but it is an important one. Your partner shouldn't give your bad behavior or bad attitude a free pass because you have insomnia.

Remember, your partner or friend also may have misconceptions about sleep. These may be due to our culture or come directly from you. For example, if you've told your partner that you're cranky because you don't sleep at night, he or she may believe this. It's important that your partner understand that although your sleep problems may affect your mood, insomnia is not 100 percent responsible for your mood. You shouldn't use your poor sleep as an excuse for not holding up your part of the relationship. If you ask your partner to take on more responsibility because you can't function due to poor sleep, eventually this will strain the relationship. Avoid this by following your normal routine and letting your partner know that this is a part of treatment. Having support for this treatment can help you achieve success.

Although we've encouraged sharing strategies and information from this workbook with others, journaling is different. Journaling is a private activity, and it's important that you write without intending to share your writing. If you plan to share your writing, this may cause you to judge, editorialize, or hold back thoughts and emotions. Rather, plan to keep your journaling in a secure place or destroy it after the writing. Some partners may question your need to withhold such information. Make sure your partner knows that keeping a private journal is an important step in facilitating your self-understanding related to sleep. However, others can still be helpful. Share what you'll be doing with your partner or another person who supports you. Ask those who are close to you if they notice a difference in you after you complete the journaling exercise. Teach others the strategies you learned in this chapter.

Teach your partner your new strategy of labeling your thoughts. Practice labeling your thoughts aloud with a willing partner. Get into the habit of using the language of cognitive defusion with those who support you.

OVERCOMING OBSTACLES AND PLANNING FOR SUCCESS

There are two common obstacles to identifying and changing beliefs about sleep. Your thoughts about sleep may be deeply entrenched from years of dealing with insomnia. You may get frustrated when you discover that understanding your beliefs doesn't change them immediately. To overcome feelings of frustration, try to remember that your thoughts will change as you master the skills found in this workbook. As you begin sleeping better, and subsequently feeling better, your thoughts will begin to change naturally because you'll be dispelling many previously held beliefs. Be patient and kind to yourself. Remember, sleeping better is a process that takes both time and effort—but it can happen for you.

The most common reason some people resist journaling is that they tried keeping a diary unsuccessfully in the past. Also, finding time to write for an uninterrupted twenty minutes can be hard, especially with all the other tasks we've asked you to do to sleep better. Remember the journaling assignment is time-limited (four sessions) and will amount to less than one and a half hours of your time. Remind yourself of your reasons for journaling (physical and mental health benefits, including falling asleep faster). Finally, remember the results you've already begun to see from using the techniques discussed here and remember that journaling will enhance the benefits to your sleep pattern.

SUGGESTED GOAL ASSIGNMENT

You've learned to examine your thoughts and beliefs about sleep. Continue using these skills to improve your sleep.

1. Monitor your sleep using the Sleep Cognitions Tracking Form.

2. Use the Task Chart to understand how insomnia affects your quality of life.

3. Journal to alleviate current stressors that may affect your sleep.

4. Observe your thoughts about sleep by identifying, challenging, and changing what you say to yourself about insomnia. Use insomnia coping statements.

5. Increase your anxiety tolerance by practicing mindfulness techniques.

Chapter 8

Understanding and Coping with Trauma-Related Nightmares

Nightmares, or distressing dreams, are a common problem for individuals with trauma-related insomnia. There are several types of nightmares and ways to both alleviate and cope with trauma-related dreams. In this chapter you will learn:

- Two types of nightmares that commonly occur following a trauma

- Ways to alleviate trauma-related nightmares

- Ways to cope following a nightmare

UNDERSTANDING DISTRESSING DREAMS

Experiencing distressing dreams while sleeping may make you feel you are not in control of your thoughts and emotions. Recurrent nightmares can make you afraid to fall asleep and may delay sleep onset.

Consider the following two examples.

◆ Elizabeth's Story

Elizabeth, twenty-two, was traveling to work one morning. She wasn't rushing. She maneuvered along a major thoroughfare at medium speeds and stopped at a red light before turning onto the road leading to her workplace. She sat in line listening to music. Then Elizabeth felt what she described as a "strange vibration on the road." She looked into her rearview mirror and saw a large truck hurtling toward her at high speed. She was struck from behind, which pushed her car into the car in front, causing her air bags to deploy.

Elizabeth sustained a broken collarbone and a concussion. Following the accident she experienced initial insomnia because of pain. Pain medications helped her to sleep, and she doesn't remember any dreams from that time. However, as she weaned herself from the medications, she started waking up from nightmares about the accident. In her dreams, she sees herself on the thoroughfare and feels vibrations before seeing the truck plowing into her car. Sometimes her nightmare varies as to who is in the car with her or what song is on the radio. Her dreams distress her. She wakes in a cold sweat and is unable to return to sleep. Also, she realizes she is more irritable for several days after she has a nightmare.

There are two important aspects to Elizabeth's story:

◆ Nightmares following a trauma vary in how closely their content links to the traumatic event. Elizabeth's nightmares closely resemble her trauma, including many of the details that occurred before and during the accident. Her dream content is trauma based.

◆ Dreams can be repetitive or nonrepetitive. Elizabeth doesn't have many versions of her nightmare. Rather, she dreams one dream again and again. The content of Elizabeth's dream is repetitive.

◆ Anne's Story

Anne, thirty-two, had dinner with friends at a restaurant near her home. After dinner, she walked home alone. Although there was less activity than usual, there were a number of people outdoors. As she was unlocking the front door to her apartment building, a man approached her from behind. He said he had a gun, and she felt the weight of it in her back. He asked for her money and jewelry and threatened to kill her if she didn't comply. Trembling, she gave him her purse and jewelry. He told her to count to one hundred before entering her home.

Anne began having nightmares immediately following this traumatic event. Although she occasionally dreams about being robbed, more often her dreams are of being threatened or chased. Her assailant varies from strangers to masked individuals to people from her past and present. She is fearful in her dreams, which awaken her. After calming herself for thirty to sixty minutes, she can usually return to sleep.

There are two important aspects to Anne's story:

- Anne's nightmares do not closely resemble her traumatic experience. They are rarely about being robbed or mugged. This doesn't mean they are not trauma-related. Anne's emotions of anxiety and fear in her dreams and the fact that the dreams began following her trauma indicate the nightmares are trauma-related.

- Anne has many variations of her dream. She doesn't dream the same, or even nearly the same, dream content every night. Her dreams are nonrepetitive in content.

Repetitive and Nonrepetitive Nightmares

Repetitive nightmares. If you didn't have nightmares before your trauma but you've had them repeatedly following the trauma, they're likely to be trauma-related. Some people with trauma-related nightmares have the same dream again and again. That is, the dream content is exactly or nearly the same in each dream. Elizabeth's dream about her accident doesn't vary much. The dream begins in the same way, nearly the same dream events occur each time, and she awakens at the same place in the dream. Her dreams are not only closely related to her traumatic event, they are repetitive in nature. That is, they repeat their content.

Nonrepetitive nightmares. Some people report they dream different content each night, even when it's about the same event. Anne's dreams about being chased and fearful are set in different places. She can be at work, at a vacation spot, or somewhere unknown. Although the emotions are the same, the details of the content of her dreams vary. Thus, her dream content is nonrepetitive.

Understanding the type of dream you have can be important for treatment. Some people have both repetitive and nonrepetitive dreams. Identify your dreams as repetitive or nonrepetitive using the guidelines below.

_____ **Repetitive:** My dreams have repetitive content. I dream the same, or nearly the same dream many nights. My dream may or may not be based specifically in my traumatic event.

_____ **Nonrepetitive:** My dream doesn't have repetitive content. Although it may be related to my traumatic event, it's not the same or nearly the same dream again and again.

Regardless of the type of nightmare you're experiencing, it's important to remember that the dream may indicate a need to process memories or emotions related to the traumatic event. This can be done with a therapist's help. There are many excellent evidence-based therapies for re-experiencing symptoms following a trauma; these therapies can help diminish both thoughts about your trauma and distressing dreams related to it. See the resources section for help finding a therapist.

ALLEVIATING TRAUMA-RELATED REPETITIVE DREAMS

If you have repetitive content dreams, a specific therapy can help to alleviate your nightmares. Techniques used in imagery rehearsal therapy (IRT; Krakow, Johnston, et al. 2001) can help you stop dreaming repetitive nightmares. IRT doesn't alleviate the memory of the event, just the distressing dream related to it. IRT works only with repetitive content nightmares. Unfortunately, there is no corresponding technique for nonrepetitive dreams. However, you can use the coping techniques described later in the chapter to cope more effectively after a distressing dream. Also, you can pursue trauma-focused therapies with a mental health professional to alleviate nonrepetitive dreams.

Imagery Rehearsal Therapy for Repetitive Nightmares

IRT can help you rid yourself of a repetitive content dream (Krakow, Johnston, et al. 2001). You should understand that dream content is different than trauma memory, even if your dream is closely related to your trauma memory. IRT cannot remove your memory of the trauma, but it can eliminate the dream related to the trauma.

Focus on one repetitive dream at a time. After IRT helps one dream, you can focus on a different dream, if needed. Use the IRT exercises below to alleviate your repetitive content nightmares.

EXERCISE: IRT Dream Account

Use the space below to write down the repetitive dream you've chosen to alleviate. Work on only one dream at a time. Include as many details as you can remember about your dream: what you see, hear, smell, touch, feel, and think in the dream. If your dream content is closely related to your trauma memory, you'll also need to focus on which details come from your nightmare rather than from the trauma event. Include only details that appear in your dream in this exercise.

RATS in LARGE underground area

Now that you've written your repetitive nightmare with as much detail as possible, you'll make a change to it. In the next exercise, rewrite your nightmare, but include a change. This change can be anywhere in your dream, but we suggest making it somewhere in the middle, neither very early nor late in the nightmare. The change can be realistic or fantastic. It doesn't necessarily have to be positive, but it should result in some relief from a distressing aspect of your dream. As you did when writing down your nightmare, be as detailed as possible in the rewriting of your dream content and the change you are making. See the examples below from individuals who used IRT to change their repetitive nightmares.

Elizabeth's repetitive dream about her accident was distressing her. She used IRT to alleviate that distress.

IRT dream account. *I'm driving my car on the highway. I'm going to work and drinking coffee out of a red travel mug. It's drizzling and I'm sleepy. I yawn. I come to a red light and stop. There are several cars in front of me. The car just in front of me is a white sedan. Its right blinker is on. My windshield wipers are squeaking in the rain. I don't like the song on the radio, and I look down to change the station. I hear a loud sound and can't figure out what it is. My heart is pounding. I look in my rearview mirror and see an 18-wheel semi barreling down on me, and then I wake up.*

IRT changed dream account. *I'm driving my car on the highway. I'm going to work and drinking coffee out of a red travel mug. It's drizzling and I feel sleepy. I yawn. I come to a red light and stop. There are several cars in front of me. The car just in front of me is a white sedan. Its right blinker is on. My windshield wipers are squeaking in the rain. I don't like the song on the radio, and I look down to change the station. I hear a loud sound and can't figure out what it is.* **I realize it's a song I really like, and I begin to snap my fingers to the beat. I sing along with the song. The light changes, and I see the car in front of me turn right. I drive straight through the green light.**

Elizabeth's change to her dream is realistic. She chose a change that could have really happened. She also could have chosen a completely fantastic scenario. For example, she could have chosen to see the 18-wheeler barreling down on her and have her car become a trampoline, catching the truck and tossing it back down the road, so that she is unharmed.

Some people find that making more fantastic changes to their nightmares is more helpful than making realistic changes. Either method can work. You can decide what feels comfortable to you. Some other examples of making changes to dreams are below. Read through these, but come up with a change that fits your nightmare and speaks to you. When you're ready, do the IRT Change Dream exercise below.

Specific Examples of Changes to Nightmares

- Bridget, a rape survivor, changed her hand into a sledgehammer and pounded her assailant into the ground.

◆ William, an auto accident survivor, chose to see his buddy fly safely out of the vehicle before it exploded.

◆ Shannon, who survived a dog attack, changed the enormous, threatening dog of her nightmare into a kitten she picked up and brought home.

◆ Clay, who survived an armed robbery, chose to have the robber's gun melt and morph into handcuffs, which allowed Clay to capture the robber.

EXERCISE: IRT Changed Dream

Use the space below to write down the repetitive nightmare you've chosen to alleviate. At some point in your dream make a change to it. Write out this change with as much detail as possible. Write what happens in the dream after the change has been made.

RATS BURNED up in FIRE

Now that you've written your changed dream, it's important that you read it every day. *Do not* read your account of your repetitive nightmare. Read the *changed dream* account as many times as you can each day and every night just before bed. The more times you read your changed dream, the faster IRT works. Read your changed dream for at least two weeks. However, for many people it takes longer than two weeks to see an effect, so keep rehearsing the changed dream until you stop dreaming your repetitive nightmare.

IRT works by eliminating your repetitive nightmare. You may find that your dreams change or that you simply stop dreaming the original nightmare. If you have several repetitive dreams, you can use the IRT technique on your second dream after you've eliminated the first.

COPING WITH NIGHTMARES

If you've been having distressing dreams following your traumatic event, whether repetitive or nonrepetitive, it's important to know how to cope with cope with them. Nightmares interfere with sleep in three ways:

1. **Nightmares cause fear about falling asleep.** You may worry you'll have a nightmare. You may be slow to fall asleep because you want to prevent a distressing dream. Such thoughts contribute to initial insomnia or an inability to fall asleep at night.

2. **Nightmares distress you while you're asleep.** They may cause awakenings during the night. You may have emotional reactions (fear, sadness, anger) or physical reactions (sweating or a pounding heartbeat) on awakening from a bad nightmare.

3. **Nightmares can prevent or delay your return to sleep following an awakening during the night.** Fears of returning to the dream or fears about having another nightmare may keep you from going back to sleep after a bad dream. The intensity of the emotions and physical reactions you have on awakening can be difficult to lessen, which also can cause difficulty in returning to sleep.

It's important to learn to cope well with nightmares so you can be confident that should one occur, you'll know how to deal with it. Learning to diminish your distress following a nightmare will allow you to return to sleep faster and more easily. Although you can use the relaxation and calm breathing strategies taught in chapters 3 and 4 to soothe yourself following a nightmare, there are some other effective tools to cope with and prevent nightmares from contributing to and worsening your insomnia.

It's important to plan what you'll do to cope with a nightmare before going to sleep. There are two strategies you can employ to help you cope: behavioral calming and emotional calming.

Behavioral Calming Following a Nightmare

It's likely that you already engage in behavioral calming techniques after awakening from a nightmare. We want to add some useful techniques to your list and have you use them from now on, to cope with distressing nightmares. These are actions you take to center yourself in the present. They help you recover more quickly from a nightmare. They get you out of bed and away from thinking about your dream.

Splashing cold water on your face or getting something to drink are examples of behavioral coping. Some behaviors will be more centering and soothing to you than others. Try many of the activities on the following list to find out which work best for you. It's possible that some of these will work better at one time, and others at other times. Knowing many behavioral calming techniques gives you more tools to choose from to soothe yourself after a distressing nightmare. Rate the effectiveness of the techniques, so you can decide which of these is most effective for you.

Behavioral Calming Techniques		
Date Used	**Technique**	**Effectiveness (0-10)**
	Taking a hot shower	/10
	Taking a cold shower	/10
	Splashing cold water on your face	/10
	Brushing your teeth	/10
	Rubbing ice on your neck and face	/10
	Drinking something cold	/10
	Drinking something hot	/10
	Stretching ✓	/10
	Other:	/10
	Other:	/10
	Other:	/10

Combining behavioral techniques can prove more useful than doing only one. Also, you can combine behavioral calming techniques with emotional techniques (listed later in the chapter). What's important is to do something other than lie in bed thinking about the nightmare, as this only prolongs your distress and prevents sleep from returning.

Emotional Calming Following a Nightmare

Emotional calming involves soothing the anxiety, anger, sadness, or other upset that remains after awakening from a nightmare. There are two ways to soothe your emotions. One way to do this is to actively conjure another, more positive, emotion. Another is to distract yourself from the upsetting emotion. Actively conjuring other, more positive emotions may be difficult. However, you'll find it becomes easier with planning and practice.

To plan to conjure an emotion, you'll need to have objects or activities at hand to arouse your emotions. These can be things to listen to, read, gaze at, or say to yourself. For example, looking at a photograph of a loved one or listening to a favorite song can provoke positive emotion. Of course, to use them when needed, you must ready them in advance by making the photograph or song easily accessible.

Healthy distraction is another emotional calming technique. It's called "healthy" because it doesn't involve methods that lead to other problems, as in alcohol or drug use. Healthy distraction engages your mind, so you stop thinking about your nightmare or trauma memory. It also keeps you from sitting for a long time with the emotions and physical reactions that awakened you from your nightmare. Healthy distraction can be anything that actively engages your mind and evokes neutral or positive emotions. For example, playing Sudoku or doing crossword puzzles can distract you. However, because these activities require paying attention to them, it's important to have simpler healthy distractions to use too.

Here are some healthy and easy distractions to try.

THE NAME GAME

To play the name game, you think of a subject you know something about (for example, tennis champions, Super Bowl winners, or types of dogs). After choosing a category, name every person, place, or thing you can think of in that category. Do this as quickly and for as long as you can. Have several categories ready to use before you go to sleep. List them below and keep the list by your bedside or in the room you typically go to after waking from a nightmare.

Name Game List

1. John Wayne Movies
2. Favorite Christmas Movies
3. Marathon Standings
4. _____
5. _____

Here is an example of a Name Game List completed by Elizabeth.

Elizabeth's Name Game List

1. *Types of birds*

2. *Cities starting with the letter M*

3. *Titles of songs by Elvis*

4. *States in alphabetical order*

5. *Students in my fourth-grade class*

ICE CUBE DISTRACTION

This is an emotional calming technique described by Gehart and McCollum (2008) and developed by Dr. Sonja Batten (forthcoming). Get a small glass of ice. Start with one ice cube and place it on various body parts (see the list below) until your attention is captured by the sensation of the ice. Focus on the feeling of the ice on each body part. What does it feel like at first? Does the feeling change? What happens to your skin? What happens to the ice? Are there differences between one body part and the next? Are you more sensitive in some places than others? You might want to talk aloud to yourself about the way the ice feels. Sometimes talking aloud can be more distracting than talking silently to yourself.

- Top of head
- Cheeks
- Side of neck
- Upper arm
- Palm
- Stomach
- Front of thigh
- Calves
- Top of feet
- Toes
- Temples
- Lips
- Chest
- Lower arm
- Back of hand
- Lower back
- Back of thigh
- Ankles
- Bottom of feet

Remember, you can combine emotional and behavioral coping by doing them together or sequentially. For example, after awakening from a nightmare, Elizabeth played the name game while taking a hot shower. After the shower, she got a cold drink. She felt emotionally calmer following these healthy distractions and returned to bed to reinitiate sleep. Before going to bed, she used the emotional and behavioral calming lists to rate their effectiveness. She rated the shower as an 8 out of 10 and the Name Game as a 9 out of 10. She rated drinking something cold as a 4 out of 10 on this night.

Try out the various emotional calming techniques below and rate their effectiveness.

Emotional Calming Techniques		
Date Used	**Technique**	**Effectiveness (0-10)**
	Using the ice technique	/10
	Using the name game	/10
	Playing Sudoku	/10
	Working a crossword puzzle	/10
	Listening to music that activates positive emotion	/10
	Looking at a photo of a loved one	/10
	Reading a calming passage or book	/10
	Watching something positive, preselected or recorded, on television	/10
	Other:	/10
	Other:	/10
	Other:	/10

Limiting the amount of time you spend thinking about nightmares upon awakening will help you to return to sleep faster. Knowing you can cope with nightmares, having behavioral and emotional calming techniques at your disposal, and having a coping plan will help to decrease any worries you have about going to sleep at night.

EXERCISE: Nightmare Coping Plan

When I awaken from a nightmare, I will do the following to promote positive emotion, distract myself emotionally and behaviorally, and soothe myself so I can return to sleep. I will engage in these activities until I feel calm.

I will…

1. WATCH RECORDING of MOVIE SERIAL

2. READING For BOOK

3.

4.

5.

MEDICATION FOR TRAUMA-RELATED NIGHTMARES

Recently, prazosin (Minipress, Vasoflex) has been used to treat trauma-related nightmares (Thompson et al. 2008; Taylor, Feeman, and Cates 2008). Some individuals find that this medication, originally used to treat high blood pressure, reduces distressing dreams following a traumatic event. No difference has been noted in repetitive versus nonrepetitive nightmares. According to the FDA, the main side effects of prazosin are dizziness, headache, drowsiness, lack of energy, weakness, palpitations, and nausea. Talk to your physician about the advantages and disadvantages of prazosin as a treatment for nightmares.

UTILIZING SUPPORT

Discuss the fact that you're having nightmares with your partner and family. You needn't discuss the content of your dreams for them to support your recovery. Discuss your Nightmare Coping Plan with your partner, too. Ask family members to help you to prepare in advance so that these strategies are available to you after awakening from a nightmare.

OVERCOMING OBSTACLES AND PLANNING FOR SUCCESS

When using imagery rehearsal therapy to eliminate repetitive nightmares, one of the biggest challenges is to stay focused while reading the changed dream. You may have it memorized after several readings, but it's essential to continue to read and imagine the changed dream as often as possible for at least two weeks. It's the repetitive rehearsal of IRT that removes your distressing nightmare.

One of the biggest obstacles to using emotional and behavioral calming techniques is failing to prepare in advance. When you awaken from a nightmare, you are disoriented and upset. This is not the time to think about a coping plan. Instead, you want to have your coping plan written down and located somewhere accessible (bedside, kitchen). Moreover, you should have any items you need already prepared. Planning in advance lets you start coping with your nightmare-related distress sooner. The sooner you begin coping, the faster you can return to sleep.

SUGGESTED GOAL ASSIGNMENT

1. Identify whether your nightmares are repetitive or nonrepetitive, or both.

2. If you have repetitive content nightmares, use IRT techniques.

3. Try behavioral calming techniques to cope after a nightmare.

4. Try emotional calming techniques to cope after a nightmare.

5. Complete a Nightmare Coping Plan and place this by your bedside or put it where you can access it easily. Discuss your Nightmare Coping Plan with your partner.

6. Update your Nightmare Coping Plan based on which behavioral and emotional calming techniques you find useful.

Chapter 9

Chronic Pain and Sleep
By Jeffrey A. West, Ph.D.

Many trauma survivors experience *chronic pain* (defined as a pain condition that persists for at least six months). If you've been dealing with pain for a long time, your coping skills and daily activities have been challenged and the situation likely contributes to your sleep difficulties. It's important to learn what we now know about chronic pain and sleep, and to use that knowledge in your nightly quest.

In this chapter you will learn about:

- Differences between acute and chronic pain

- Chronic pain conditions

- Pain as a complex perceptual experience

- Impacts of chronic pain on sleep

- Pain medications and sleep

DIFFERENCES BETWEEN ACUTE AND CHRONIC PAIN

The ability to perceive pain has many positive benefits. Pain serves as a signal that something is wrong. It's effective because it is difficult to ignore and triggers changes in thoughts, feelings, and actions. Most of the usefulness of pain derives from what is called *acute pain*, which is pain that comes on quickly as a response to a specific circumstance, like an injury or infection. Acute pain can be severe, disruptive, even debilitating. It lasts a relatively short time and typically responds to treatment. As its cause is corrected, it tends to resolve. Like a functioning smoke detector, it's unpleasant when activated but can save your life.

Sometimes pain becomes *chronic*. This means it persists over time, resists change, and may be poorly coordinated with changes in the condition that started it or with treatments that might be effective for acute pain. Although both acute and chronic pain can disrupt sleep, chronic pain is more formidable due to its longer duration and more pervasive effects.

◆ *Candace and Chronic Pain*

Candace's difficulties with pain and sleep began five years ago following an accident on her job at a construction site, when she fell from a moving crane and dislocated her shoulder. She recalls feeling helpless and frightened, along with the most intense pain she'd ever experienced. Since then, she's had surgery and physical therapy and has regained much use of her right arm. Most days, she continues to perceive moderate pain in her arm and shoulder, with regular flare-ups of severe pain, sometimes lasting several days. She has used pain medications with mixed effectiveness, and on many occasions her shoulder has "come out of its socket." At those times, she experiences severe pain and flashbacks to the original injury. She feels apprehensive using her arm now and is worried she'll dislocate her shoulder again.

Candace experienced severe acute pain immediately following her injury. Do you agree that her more chronic pain represents a bigger threat to her quality of life? Do you see how Candace's pain now is like an erratic smoke detector that goes off too often?

CHRONIC PAIN CONDITIONS

Chronic pain is associated with many common medical conditions, including diabetes, arthritis, neuropathy, and neck, back, or joint injuries. It also correlates with clinical depression, anxiety, and post-traumatic difficulties. With these conditions, people generally experience sleep difficulties along with chronic pain.

◆ *Candace's Chronic Pain and Sleep*

For five years, Candace has thought her sleep impaired. She dreads going to bed, expecting the night will be hard to endure. She says, "Sometimes, I feel defeated before I've even started trying to go to sleep." She feels tense and tight, her pain spreading. Late at night, she watches movies and eats to avoid bedtime. She tries sitting calmly in a chair to reduce tension but often finds the more she tries to relax, the more her shoulder hurts. When she does lie down, it's hard to get comfortable, especially in certain positions. She tries to lie as still as possible. Her shoulder usually aches and, occasionally, she feels sharp internal jabs both when she moves and when she stays still too long. In bed she tosses and turns for long periods but is afraid to get up.

She worries about her shoulder "popping out" again. She reviews her life and how it changed after her injury. She thinks about the accident and what she might have done differently. She's noticed that she's always tired, night and day, but cannot relieve this by sleeping soundly. Previously, Candace had always seen herself as a strong person; now she wonders how this could have happened to her.

PAIN AS A COMPLEX PERCEPTUAL EXPERIENCE

Before examining the relationship between chronic pain and sleep, it's important to recognize a key point about the experience of pain as currently understood. We refer to pain as *perceived pain* to emphasize that both acute and chronic pain reflect complex perceptual experiences rather than simple sensory ones.

Your brain creates the experiences called "pain" from many possible inputs and outputs along your central nervous system and throughout your body. Pain signals may be amplified, blocked, or diverted in varying combinations depending on multiple factors, boosting or suppressing the pain ultimately experienced. Pain, in turn, affects and is affected by the functioning of your body, emotional state, ongoing activity, and behavior. You can take medications that will affect pain processing at various locations in your nervous system, but you can also change the focus, attention, and cognitive activity of your brain to decrease or magnify your experience of pain.

Sleep is highly vulnerable to chronic pain and is affected by many factors influenced by pain, including attention, relaxation, worry, emotionality, cognition, and association. You can use various strategies to affect these factors and enhance your sleep. Each area impacted by pain also provides you with an opportunity to enhance your ability to cope with pain, and thus enhance the quality of your sleep.

IMPACTS OF CHRONIC PAIN ON SLEEP

You may have recognized some of your own experiences in Candace's nightly struggles and noticed negative impacts of chronic pain on your sleep. Your pain sensations may interfere with processes in your body that initiate and maintain sleep. The emotional, cognitive, and physiological reactions to pain's insistent (and no longer helpful) signals promote thoughts, feelings, and behaviors that interfere with sleeping well.

Like Candace, you are vulnerable to pain-related impacts from many factors affecting sleep, such as your preparation for bed; bedtime activities; effects of position and movement; worries about your life; and sense of lack of control. Also, your chronic pain may interfere with thoughts and behaviors that formerly promoted sleep.

If your challenges with pain and sleep are multifaceted like Candace's, you may want to use "personal tools" to influence different aspects of your body, mind, and behavior. These include strategies to reduce arousal and promote relaxation and tools to change other aspects of your sleeping environment, which, when combined, have demonstrated effectiveness (National Institutes of Health 1996; Currie et al. 2000). When a factor affected by pain is identified, altering that factor may work toward lessened impact of the pain.

APPLY YOUR KNOWLEDGE TO IMPROVE SLEEP WITH CHRONIC PAIN

The strategies to promote sleep described in earlier chapters also apply to efforts to improve poor sleep associated with chronic pain. These efforts include strategies for calming your body and mind, redirecting your thinking, and improving your environment in ways that will promote better sleep. Altering your perception of pain when possible will also be helpful. Rather than repeat information discussed earlier, this chapter highlights some details particularly relevant to sleeping with chronic pain.

Relaxation and Chronic Pain

As you've learned, having a relaxed mind and body is key to the ability to sleep, yet in the face of chronic pain, this is difficult to achieve. Experiment regularly with the progressive muscle relaxation, self-hypnosis, and autogenic relaxation techniques you learned in chapter 4. With chronic pain, individual responses can be variable, so it's important to determine which approach works best for you and to customize the details to increase their effectiveness in helping you cope with your perceived pain.

For many, progressive muscle relaxation is very helpful for coping with chronic pain, but be aware that decreases in muscle tension sometimes increase the perception of pain, especially in certain positions. For example, Candace experiences increased pain in her shoulder while sitting in a chair because sitting produces increased strain on the affected areas of her shoulder. The solution could involve lying down or supporting her arms better while sitting.

Experiment with changes in posture and positioning. Note that muscle relaxation may provide you with the greatest benefit through the reduction of secondary pains, which are generated in areas that weren't injured, rather than greatly reducing pain sensations in the original pain site. The muscles of Candace's upper back and neck "guard" or brace her sensitive shoulder throughout the day and night, staying tight to reduce shocks to the injury area. When these muscles became chronically tight (to the point of spasm), the discomfort interfered with her sleep as much or more than her painful shoulder. Progressive muscle relaxation training can provide great benefit in such situations. When you scan your feelings throughout your body while practicing progressive muscle relaxation, you'll discover whether this applies to you, too.

Self-Hypnosis, Calm Breathing, and Autogenic Relaxation

You may find that self-hypnosis, calm breathing, and autogenic relaxation approaches fit better with your efforts to calm body and mind, compared to direct muscle manipulation. Practice these techniques with a focus on breathing, warmth, or heaviness in your extremities to explore whether they seem less sensitizing or pain-provoking. Calm breathing can be done in almost any setting and may provide the foundation of your calming efforts when other strategies are difficult.

Guided Imagery

In guided imagery, relaxation is combined with visualization techniques to increase effectiveness. *Visualization* refers to using your imagination to picture images in your mind's eye that promote mental and physical calmness, coping, and health. When you do this in a relaxed state, your mind's reaction to the alarm signal of perceived pain is altered, and you can guide yourself through imagery toward more positive or helpful states.

EXERCISE: Visualization

Explore your visualization potential while you're in a comfortable position and responding to calm breathing or other relaxation approaches. With eyes gently closed, notice the images you see in your mind. Initially, there may be light or dark patterns or specific patterns or images, or your mind's eye may see a dark, velvet curtain. When you become aware of the images in your mind, whatever they are, try to picture, as vividly as possible, a beautiful tree.

Let yourself see details of the tree that comes to mind. Examine it, first from a distance. Then come closer to the tree as you visualize it in greater detail. Look up into the branches overhead, then down at the roots entering the ground. Examine the bark at eye level. Notice its texture. Imagine what it would feel like to reach out and run your hands over it. Experience as fully as you can all the details of the image. When you're ready, open your eyes and examine how you feel.

Has the visualization led you to experience your present state differently in any way? Did it provide a brief diversion from your earlier frame of mind? I've found that visualizing a tree often helps get people started using this technique. Moreover, it can lead to other images as you continue practicing; for example, by visualizing yourself circling the tree and stepping into another visualized environment.

Guided imagery is a dual process: first you achieve a state of deep relaxation through focusing on slow breathing and releasing tension in your body, then you introduce your visualized images and guide yourself through them. There is no limit to the imagery you can explore to assist your body and mind to prepare for sleep.

You can focus on your pain itself. One technique has you generate a mental image of your pain to observe it, then you transform the image by shrinking it, throwing it away, locking it into a confined place, or watching it evaporate. Then allow pleasant drowsiness to begin. You can also create an image of a pain-intensity knob, which you can turn to alter your perception. You can even visualize images that remove you from your perception of pain by placing you in a very comfortable, distracting, or pleasing environment. It is well worth the effort to seek and create images that are especially potent or natural for you. Because pain perceptions are highly individualized, you may discover that some images and sensations are especially effective and others are not.

Pain-consistent and pain-inconsistent images. In this context, "consistency" refers to having your guided image correspond to specific sensations of your pain perceptions, as opposed to counteracting or contradicting those sensations. Experiment with differences between pain-consistent and pain-inconsistent images; you may find one approach easier or more effective than the other. For example, if you experience "hot" neuropathic pain in your feet and legs, try relaxing heat-related images of sunlight or warm tropical water bathing your feet (a pain-consistent image). Later, try using an image of playing in the cold snow on a beautiful winter day (a pain-inconsistent image, with pleasurable cold counteracting "hot" pain perceptions).

Activate all your senses. Note that you may respond best to images that incorporate many sensory modalities, not just singular ones. For example, while visualizing yourself lying on a beach relaxing, try to incorporate the feel of balmy breeze on your skin, the sound of waves breaking against sand, and the warmth of sunlight caressing your skin. Try to activate all your senses as much as possible, rather than simply picturing yourself lying on a beach.

Images to promote security. Another technique you may find especially powerful uses images that promote feelings of security. These images can help counter the danger-signal aspect of chronic pain and the memories of traumatic events, which may occur while you lie quietly trying to fall asleep. If you can develop and use imagery accompanied by feelings of enhanced security, safety, or shelter, over time this can become increasingly effective at promoting better sleep.

You'll have to explore the possibilities to find what works for you. Candace, for example, likes to visualize being in a warm, dry cabin with steady rain falling outside. Other examples include wearing a magic cloak that renders anyone who wears it invisible and impervious to harm. Such images can be visualized as places where pain shrinks or fades. With use, safety images can trigger the process of letting go and automatically promote the desire for sleep.

For all calming and relaxation techniques, keep in mind that their purpose extends beyond achieving a calm state to promote sleep (although that is a worthwhile goal). You can also think of these techniques as conditioning exercises to help your body make the transition between tension and relaxation easier. Practicing these techniques will help you more clearly identify the state of tension or calmness that you experience at any given time. Regular practice will help you to recognize tension at earlier stages and signal you to begin using your relaxation tools for improving sleep. For example, hours before bedtime, you may become better at detecting rising stress. You may deal with stress better earlier in the day than when it reaches maximum levels later.

The Bedroom Environment and Overcoming Chronic Pain

The overall environment of your bedroom is vital to your efforts to reduce insomnia, particularly when you're coping with chronic pain. Many aspects of your environment can be fine-tuned to reduce triggering discomfort. For example, proper head and neck support with a pillow that increases your comfort can make a significant difference in your ability to fall and remain asleep. Mattress firmness is another variable that can have a profound impact on both pain and comfort.

Pay attention to factors like temperature, lighting, and sound. Remember, you are likely to be more sensitive to and potentially disrupted by changing levels of light, sound, and temperature than by steady levels. For this reason, you may sleep better with a moderate but steady noise, rather than trying to achieve silence. You can add constant white noise (for example, a steady running fan, a low-volume radio station, or ambient music) to your bedroom to reduce sleep disruptions caused by unanticipated noise. This is especially true for those with chronic pain, because pain may promote and sustain hypersensitivity to environmental disruptions. Pain may also be associated with microarousals, or brief awakenings, that disrupt sleep. Eliminating potentially disruptive elements from your bedroom will improve your ability to fall and stay asleep and increase your ability to deal with other sleep impediments caused by chronic pain.

Redirecting Your Mind: Coexisting with Chronic Pain

When chronic pain cannot be eliminated, it's vital to consider ways that will enable you to coexist with it, as an essential part of coping. This can be an unfamiliar and unwelcome challenge, quite different from your efforts to find effective ways to decrease the intensity of your pain. Unfortunately, the pain-relieving approach may not be available to you or may be subject to side effects and setbacks.

It can be liberating to explore the possibility that some level of pain can be accepted as an unwanted but present part of life, and that you can continue pursuing goals despite the presence of pain. You can use the tools you learned in chapter 7 to identify and challenge your thoughts and beliefs about your chronic pain. People with chronic pain often struggle with feelings of loss, anger, frustration, and hopelessness. Although these emotions are normal, you may be able to decrease their intensity by examining your thoughts and beliefs. (See the resources section for books that can help with this approach.)

PAIN MEDICATIONS AND SLEEP

Many types of medications are used to manage chronic pain conditions. These include both over-the-counter and prescription drugs. Over-the-counter medications include acetaminophen, aspirin, and other nonsteroidal anti-inflammatory drugs (NSAIDs), such as ibuprofen and naproxen sodium. Topical creams containing corticosteroids, capsaicin, menthol, aspirin, and other compounds that can affect pain transmission and alter inflammation are also common.

Prescription medications include various opioids, which alter pain perception via actions in the central nervous system, more powerful corticosteroids, and anticonvulsants (commonly employed to reduce neuropathic pain). Antidepressants like amitriptyline (Elavil), citalopram (Celexa), duloxetine (Cymbalta), or trazodone (Desyrel) may be prescribed for their potential to reduce pain and help sleep. Prescription muscle relaxers like cyclobenzaprine (Flexeril) and benzodiazepines such as diazepam (Valium) may be utilized to decrease primary and secondary muscle pain associated with certain chronic pain conditions.

It's clear that medications have an important place in treating chronic pain, and they can improve sleep in certain circumstances. This may be due to direct reduction in perceived pain that results in less interference with sleep, as with effective opioid therapy; or due to impacts on sleep-regulating systems and pain inhibition, as with antidepressants. Moreover, many of the medications above promote drowsiness and a general sedation that helps with sleep onset.

Note that there are important differences between immediate-release, or short-acting, medications, and timed-release, also known as controlled-release (CR), sustained-release (SR), and extended-release (ER, XR, or XL) medications. Immediate-release medications become available and pharmacologically active in the body relatively soon after you take them, with pain-reducing effects typically starting within fifteen to thirty minutes, peaking in approximately ninety minutes to two hours, then ending after approximately four hours.

Timed-release medications typically remain at active levels for six to twelve hours and offer the advantage of a less frequent dose schedule when medications are taken daily, as well as fewer fluctuations in their effects. Immediate-release medications are generally preferred for intermittent use based on variable needs, whereas timed-release medications are most often prescribed when a more continuous, preemptive reduction in pain is needed.

Although various pain medications can help to improve sleep under some circumstances, many of these can impact the specifics of your sleep significantly, including the proportion of time spent in the different stages of sleep. This can affect the restful or restorative quality of your sleep. A few of these effects are summarized in the table below.

The Impact of Pain Medications on the Stages of Sleep

Stage of Sleep	Summary Description of Stage	Possible Medication Effects
1	Drowsiness; feels like transition between sleeping and waking; you may not recognize you're beginning to sleep	◆ OTC medications may increase drowsiness. ◆ Anticonvulsants and anti-depressants can increase drowsiness. ◆ Benzodiazepine withdrawal can worsen insomnia. ◆ Benzodiazepines can increase stage 1 sleep at the expense of stage 5.
2	Start of deeper sleep; very short	
3	Deep sleep; associated with restorative aspects of sleep	◆ Opioids can reduce the amount of deep sleep, decreasing the restfulness and restorative quality of sleep.
4	Deep sleep; more intense than stage 3; most restorative	
5	Rapid eye movement (REM) sleep; later in sleep cycle; dreaming occurs	◆ Benzodiazepines and opioids can reduce the amount of REM sleep.

It's important to know that one or more of your pain-related medications can have a variety of impacts on your sleep. Evaluate both the quality and the amount of sleep you get when you use specific medicines, and avoid assumptions. You should monitor and record summary information for these medications, including the timing or scheduling of your doses, by using the Nightly Sleep Tracking Form (see chapter 2). This information is useful to you and your physician as an important element of your overall response to medication.

OVERCOMING OBSTACLES AND PLANNING FOR SUCCESS

Chronic pain can aggravate and complicate your insomnia, but there are many things you can do to achieve better sleep despite persistent pain. Additionally, you should be aware of factors that potentially may worsen your insomnia, including certain pain medications taken close to bedtime.

The most pressing challenge of chronic pain is its relentless persistence, with no prospect of end or cure. The need to respond to this, to draw repeatedly on strategies that provide temporary relief but no permanent resolution, may be your most significant obstacle. To address sleep problems caused by chronic pain, you must play an active role and develop a varied skill set to maximize your ability to affect those parts of your chronic pain that you have some control over, and to lessen the negative impacts of those parts that you cannot affect. It's essential to have a sense of your progress toward these goals and to appreciate the accomplishments you've already achieved. I hope that this chapter will start you thinking about varied approaches and will inspire you to try and use new strategies to promote sleep despite chronic pain.

Chapter 10

Staying Motivated: Making Treatment Work

It can be difficult to stay motivated to change your sleep habits. Too often, it's easier to do what you know than what you don't know, because change is not always comfortable. But when you purchased this workbook, you made a commitment to change your sleep pattern. To remain motivated to change it's important to stay focused on your sleep problems, remember your reasons for wanting change, and examine any obstacles that may interfere with this change. Let's consider Georgia's example.

◆ *Georgia's Story*

Georgia, thirty-nine, is married. She's had insomnia since being in a car accident five years ago. In the past, she tried sleep medications, which worked initially but stopped working. Occasionally, she uses alcohol to sleep and naps during the day.

Five weeks ago Georgia began using the techniques in this workbook. Some strategies in the workbook sounded more useful than others, so she decided to implement only those. She chose to ignore the fifteen-minute rule, continued napping during the day, and didn't remove the television or weapons from her bedroom. Her sleep improved a little, but not as much as she had hoped it would.

Then Georgia's husband read the introduction to this workbook. He pointed out to Georgia that it's the total of all the techniques that leads to the best results. Georgia remembered reading this. She decided to use the strategies from this chapter to examine her reasons for change and the obstacles stopping her from changing.

Georgia decided that her sleep problems were causing significant difficulties in her life, so she finally implemented the techniques she'd previously avoided and ultimately overcame her sleep problems.

These are the important points in Georgia's story:

◆ She worked hard on some strategies but not on others.

◆ Using a few techniques, she made some improvement to her sleep but not as much as she'd hoped.

◆ To overcome her trauma-related insomnia, she had to re-examine her sleep, her reasons for wanting better sleep, and the obstacles keeping her from using all of the techniques.

SLEEP PROBLEM REVIEW

If you're having trouble implementing the techniques in this workbook, it's important to reassess your sleep problems. Examine your Nightly Sleep Tracking Form (chapter 2) to assess your current sleep quality and quantity. Ask yourself how important it is for you to improve your sleep at this time. It may help to use a scale of 0 to 10, with 10 being most important.

Overall, how important is it to improve your sleep at this time? __10__ /10

This should provide a good estimate of your sleep and how much you'd like to change it. However, when trying to motivate yourself to change such complex, challenging issues, analyzing the problem may not be enough. Examining how much or how little you sleep may be less helpful than exploring how sleep (or its lack) affects your life. Understanding your values (the most significant guiding aspects of your life) and how sleep interferes with them can be an important way to motivate change and reinforce commitment to overcoming insomnia. Using principles developed by Miller and Rollnick (2002), this chapter will help you to examine your reasons for changing sleep patterns, your confidence in your ability to make changes, and the strengths you have that will help you to be successful. Use the Understanding Reasons for Change Form below to examine how sleep problems interfere with your life.

Understanding Reasons for Change Form

1. What are the most significant people, activities, or things in your life? List them and rate their significance from 0 (not significant) to 10 (very significant).

Value	Significance Rating
a. WIFE / KIDS	____/10
b. FITNESS \ RUNNING	____/10
c. PERSONAL PROJECTS	____/10

2. How does your insomnia interfere with your values or ability to live in accord with them?

a. LOWER ENERGY

b.

c.

3. How would this be different if you were sleeping better?

MORE ENERGY

4. If you decide to live more in accord with your values, how confident are you that you will succeed? Rate your confidence from 0 (not confident) to 10 (extremely confident).

Value 7₀	Confidence Rating
a.	7-8/10

b.	*9* /10
c.	*7-8* /10

5. If your confidence rating is a 1/10 or higher for value (a), write some sentences about what this confidence is based on and why you have this confidence.

MENTAL outlook an Future

If your confidence rating is a 1/10 or higher for value (b), write some sentences about what this confidence is based on and why you have this confidence.

MORE physical endurance

If your confidence rating is a 1/10 or higher for value (c), write some sentences about what this confidence level is based on and why you have this confidence.

MENTAL outlook

6. What strengths can you can draw upon to make changes to your sleep? Think about tough changes you've made in the past and what helped you then. What qualities do you have that can help you to change?

a.	*DED DETERMINATION — never give up*
b.	*it = worth trying board break*
c.	*determin — hopeful*

Georgia used the Understanding Reasons for Change Form to examine her reasons for wanting to change her sleep pattern. She then decided to implement more techniques from this workbook based on her desire to change and belief that she could change.

Georgia's Understanding Reasons for Change Form

1. Name the most significant people, activities, or things in your life. List them and rate their significance from 0 (not significant) to 10 (very significant).

Value	Significance Rating
a. *My family relationships* w'FC,)T ihs	10/10
b. *Doing a good job at work* ~ Λη οΦη,	10/10
c. *Giving to others* ητΤς ―	10/10

2. How does your insomnia interfere with your values or ability to live in accord with them?

Lνch ιↄf   ρφ }ℓↄↄ   ―   ↄ ↄ υℓↄↄↄↄ

a. *My family relationships: My husband and daughter say I'm cranky. I nap instead of playing with my child. I don't do activities because I'm too tired.*

b. *Doing a good job at work: I don't enjoy work because I'm tired. I'm sleepy at work because I want to nap.*   E n ɛ n q ч

c. *Giving to others: I haven't done much charity work since my accident, due to poor sleep. I'm just too tired to do this, although I really want to.*

3. How would this be different if you were sleeping better?

I've learned that if I slept better, I'd want to be more active and if I were more active, even though I'm tired, it would improve my life. It might also help me to sleep. I might feel better about myself, my work, and enjoy giving to others again.

4. If you decide to live more in accord with your values, how confident are you that you will succeed? Rate your confidence from 0 (not confident) to 10 (extremely confident).

8 - 10

Value	Confidence Rating
a. *My family relationships*	8/10
b. *Doing a good job at work*	10/10
c. *Giving to others*	5/10

5. If your confidence rating is a 1/10 or higher for value (a), write some sentences about what this confidence level is based on and why you have this confidence.

I'm 8/10 confident because my family is so important to me. I want to be there for them, and I can't let my sleep problems prevent me from doing things with them.

If your confidence rating is a 1/10 or higher for value (b), write some sentences about what this confidence level is based on and why you have this confidence.

I'm 10/10 confident because I know I do a good job at work. If I sleep better, I might do better. I'm still very successful. If I cut out some bad sleep habits to sleep better, I'd enjoy work more.

If your confidence rating is a 1/10 or higher for value (c), write some sentences about what this confidence level is based on and why you have this confidence.

I'm 5/10 confident in this because in the past when I've put my mind to tasks, I've accomplished them. If I try to do this, I think I'll succeed.

6. What strengths can you draw upon to make changes to your sleep? Think about tough changes you've made in the past and what helped you then. What qualities do you have that can help you to change?

a. *I've made tougher changes to my life before.*

b. *I survived a trauma; I can survive anything.*

c. *I really want to sleep better.*

The last step to overcoming problems while engaging in treatment for insomnia is to examine your personal obstacles. The Overcoming Obstacles sections of each chapter were designed to help you overcome common problems. It's also important to examine what specifically prevents you from engaging in treatment. Take some time to think about this next question:

What is the worst that can happen if you use _15 min rule_ ? (List any technique you haven't used; for example, the fifteen-minute rule or removing the TV from the bedroom.) Do this for each technique you have not tried to implement.

Your answer:

15 min rule = be alone tired at least resting if resting is resting in bed

_____

_____

_____

_____

_____

_____

_____

_____

When working with people struggling to overcome insomnia after a traumatic event, we've found that unhelpful or unbalanced beliefs (see chapter 7) often prevent them from trying various techniques. Insomnia after a trauma can be a self-perpetuating problem. The symptoms of trauma-related insomnia keep you from doing things to help yourself overcome it. Examine your answer to the question above. Does it resemble any of the common answers below?

Common Answers

◆ The techniques won't work. They'll be a waste of my time and effort.

◆ I'll discover my sleep problems are unfixable.

◆ I might fail.

◆ I'll find out something is really wrong with me.

◆ I'll become overwhelmed.

◆ The techniques will make my sleep problems worse.

If any of these answers resonate with you, it may be that your unhelpful insomnia-related thinking prevents you from trying the strategies and techniques in this workbook to overcome your sleep problems. Just as in chapter 7, you can challenge your thinking to develop more balanced thoughts and expectations about your ability to overcome insomnia. Use the worksheet below to challenge these unhelpful thoughts. If you need to review how to do these thought challenging techniques, review chapter 7.

Challenge Your Unhelpful Thoughts Worksheet

My Beliefs or Thoughts About Insomnia Treatment	Resulting Emotion or Mood	Coping Statement	New Emotion or Mood

Georgia used this exercise to examine her beliefs about the treatment. See her completed exercise below.

Georgia's Challenge Your Unhelpful Thoughts Worksheet			
My Beliefs or Thoughts about Insomnia Treatment	**Resulting Emotion or Mood**	**Coping Statement**	**New Emotion or Mood**
The techniques won't work. This will be a waste of time and effort.	*Anxiety, worry, frustration*	*I don't know that these won't work for me. I haven't given them a real chance.*	*Hope, concern*
I might fail.	*Depressed*	*I might not fail. Even if I don't get a perfect night's sleep, I might sleep better than I have for five years. If I don't try, I won't know.*	*Relief*
It will make my sleep problems worse.	*Upset, dejected*	*My sleep problems aren't getting better on their own. I want to sleep better. Maybe this will help.*	*Motivated*

We've seen people begin sleeping better by using the techniques in this book following a traumatic event. If you're reading this chapter, chances are your sleep hasn't improved as much as you were hoping. Perhaps you've encountered obstacles that kept you from fully implementing all of the techniques in the book. However, if you use this chapter to overcome any barriers you have to using the techniques, and you make sure to implement the techniques in the consistent and prolonged way discussed in earlier chapters, you'll begin to see real improvement in your sleep. We know you can do it! Get motivated to sleep better today.

Appendix

Treatment Checklist

A checklist of techniques discussed in this workbook appears below. Use this list to ensure that you incorporate all the techniques into your sleep therapy routines.

Chapter 1: Trauma-Related Sleep Problems

_____ Learn about normal sleep, insomnia, and sleep problems following a traumatic event.

Chapter 2: Assessing Your Sleep Pattern, Setting Goals, and Getting Started

_____ Increase your understanding of your sleep pattern by completing the Trauma Insomnia Quiz.

_____ Begin to track your sleep using the Nightly Sleep Tracking Form.

_____ Ask yourself important questions about your sleep.

_____ If you have a partner, ask him or her questions about your sleep and the impact it has on his or her sleep. Have your partner help you track your sleep using the Nightly Sleep Tracking Form, so you'll have more information.

_____ Set realistic goals for yourself using the Sleep Goals Checklist and share your goals with your partner.

Chapter 3: Your Bedroom Is for Sleep: De-Stress It!

_____ Practice calm breathing ten minutes a day.

_____ Identify and move wakeful activities outside the bedroom. Reserve your bedroom for sleep and sex only.

_____ Limit your sleep to the bedroom. Do not sleep in any other room.

_____ Avoid daytime napping, or limit it to one twenty-minute nap before 2 p.m.

_____ Use the Energy Level Tracking Worksheet, if needed, to identify the times you are at risk for napping.

_____ Reduce hypervigilance (extreme watchfulness) in your bedroom, including weapon removal, if needed.

_____ Use the Weapons in the Bedroom Evaluation to decide whether having a weapon in the bedroom affects your sleep.

_____ Use self-soothing statements.

_____ Use the Weapon Removal Change Form to move your weapons from the bedroom for a better night's sleep.

_____ Follow the fifteen-minute rule every night, and use My Relaxing Place Plan.

Chapter 4: Prepare Your Body and Mind for Sleep

_____ Practice relaxation training (RT) using the strategy of your choice for fifteen minutes or more each day. Practice during the day when awake and at night as part of your wind-down routine.

_____ Put the day to rest early each evening in a room other than your bedroom.

_____ Practice your own bedtime wind-down routine every night at the same time.

_____ Avoid late-night television or any other media that arouses you in any manner.

Chapter 5: Help Yourself to a Good Night's Sleep

____ Identify and change habits and preferences that interfere with sleep, including the following:

    ____ Caffeine

    ____ Alcohol

    ____ Nicotine

    ____ Diet

    ____ Exercise

____ Optimize your surroundings for a good night's sleep, including identifying and making changes as needed to:

    ____ Noise level

    ____ Lighting

    ____ Room temperature

    ____ Air quality

    ____ Bed comfort

    ____ Clothing choices

____ Use the Environment and Sleep Compromise Worksheet to address changes with your bed partner.

Chapter 6: Time to Sleep: Sleep Scheduling

____ Understand your sleep better by using the Total Sleep Time Tracking Worksheet.

____ Set a morning awakening time.

____ Determine your appropriate bedtime.

____ Follow your sleep plan every night.

____ Add to your sleep if needed.

Chapter 7: Sleep Beliefs: How You Think Affects How You Sleep

_____ Monitor your sleep using the Sleep Cognitions Tracking Form.

_____ Use the Task Chart to understand how insomnia affects your participation in daily life.

_____ Write in your journal to alleviate current stressors that may be affecting your sleep.

_____ Observe your thoughts about sleep by identifying, challenging, and changing what you say to yourself about insomnia. Use insomnia coping statements.

_____ Increase your anxiety tolerance by practicing mindfulness techniques.

Chapter 8: Understanding and Coping With Trauma-Related Nightmares

_____ Identify whether your nightmares are repetitive or nonrepetitive.

_____ Use imagery rehearsal therapy (IRT) if you have repetitive content nightmares.

_____ Try behavioral and emotional calming techniques to cope after a nightmare.

_____ Complete a Nightmare Coping Plan and place this by your bedside or somewhere you can access it easily. Discuss your Nightmare Coping Plan with your partner.

_____ Update your Nightmare Coping Plan based on the behavioral and emotional calming techniques you find useful.

Chapter 9: Chronic Pain and Sleep

_____ Identify differences between acute and chronic pain.

_____ Understand pain as a complex perceptual experience.

_____ Identify ways to address effects of chronic pain on sleep.

_____ Assess impact of pain medications on sleep.

Resources

If additional help is needed in the following areas, here is a list of resources.

Locating mental health professionals

American Psychological Association (APA). www.apa.org

Association for Behavioral and Cognitive Therapies (ABCT). www.abct.org

Anxiety Disorders Association of America (ADAA). www.adaa.org

National Register of Health Service Providers in Psychology. www.nationalregister.org

Quitting smoking

National Cancer Institute. www.smokefree.gov. (800) 422-6237

Centers for Disease Control (CDC). www.cdc.gov/tobacco/quit_smoking/index.htm

Nicotine Anonymous. www.nicotine-anonymous.org/

American Heart Association. (800)-242-8721

Chronic pain

Lewandowski, M. J. 2006. *The Chronic Pain Care Workbook: A Self-Treatment Approach to Pain Relief Using the Behavioral Assessment of Pain Questionnaire.* Oakland, CA. New Harbinger Publications.

Dahl, J., and T. Lundgren. 2006. *Living Beyond Your Pain: Using Acceptance and Commitment Therapy to Ease Chronic Pain.* Oakland, CA. New Harbinger Publications.

American Pain Foundation. www.painfoundation.org

References

Acierno, R. A., D. G. Kilpatrick, H. S. Resnick, B. E. Saunders, and C. L. Best. 1996. Violent assault, posttraumatic stress disorder, and depression: Risk factors for cigarette use among adult women. *Behavior Modification* 20: 363-384.

American Academy of Sleep Medicine. 2009. Insomnia. www.sleepeducation.com/Disorder. aspx?id=6. Accessed March 15, 2010.

American Psychiatric Association. 2000. *Diagnostic and Statistical Manual of Mental Disorders* (4th ed., text revision). Washington, DC: American Psychiatric Association.

Batten, S. V. Forthcoming. *Essentials of Acceptance and Commitment Therapy.* London: Sage Publications.

Beck, A. T., A. J. Rush, B. F. Shaw, and G. Emery. 1979. *Cognitive Therapy for Depression.* New York: Guilford Press.

Bootzin, R. R., and D. R. Epstein. 2000. Stimulus control. In *Treatment of Late-Life Insomnia,* edited by K. L. Lichstein and C. M. Morin. Thousand Oaks, CA: Sage Publications.

Currie, S. R., K. G. Wilson, A. J. Pontefract, and L. dePlante. 2000. Cognitive-behavioral treatment of insomnia secondary to chronic pain. *Journal of Consulting and Clinical Psychology* 68: 407-416.

Davis, M., E. Eshelman, and M. McKay. 2008. *The Relaxation and Stress Reduction Workbook.* Oakland, CA: New Harbinger Publications.

Engdahl, B. E., R. E. Eberly, T. D. Hurwitz, M. W. Mahowald, and J. D. Blake. 2000. Sleep in a community sample of elderly war veterans with and without posttraumatic stress disorder. *Biological Psychiatry* 47: 520-525.

Foa, E., and B. O. Rothbaum. 2001. *Treating the Trauma of Rape.* New York: Guilford Press.

Gehart, D., and E. E. McCollum. 2008. Inviting therapeutic presence: A mindfulness-based approach. In *Mindfulness and the Therapeutic Relationship*, edited by S. F. Hick and T. Bien. New York: Guilford Press.

Harvey, A. G. 2000. Pre-sleep cognitive activity in insomnia: A comparison of sleep onset insomniacs and good sleepers. *British Journal of Clinical Psychology* 38: 401-405.

Harvey, A. G., and R. A. Bryant. 1998. The relationship between acute stress disorder and posttraumatic stress disorder: A prospective evaluation of motor vehicle accident survivors. *Journal of Consulting and Clinical Psychology* 66: 507-512.

Harvey, A. G., and C. Farrell. 2003. The efficacy of a Pennebaker-like writing intervention for poor sleepers. *Behavioral Sleep Medicine* 1: 115-124.

Harvey, A. G., N. K. Y. Tang, and L. Browning. 2005. Cognitive approaches to insomnia. *Clinical Psychology Review* 25: 593-611.

Hauri, P., and S. Linde. 1996. *No More Sleepless Nights.* New York: John Wiley & Sons.

Hayes, S. C., with S. Smith. 2005. *Get Out of Your Mind and Into Your Life: The New Acceptance and Commitment Therapy.* Oakland, CA: New Harbinger Publications.

Hayes, S. C., K. D. Strosahl, and K. G. Wilson. 1999. *Acceptance and Commitment Therapy: An Experiential Approach to Behavior Change.* New York: Guilford Press.

Kessler, R. C., A. Sonnega, E. Bromet, M. Hughes, and C. B. Nelson. 1995. Posttraumatic stress disorder in the National Comorbidity Survey. *Archives of General Psychiatry* 52: 1048-1060.

King, A. C., R. F. Oman, G. S. Brassington, D. L. Bliwise, W. L. Haskell. 1997. Moderate-intensity exercise and self-rated quality of sleep in older adults: A randomized controlled trial. *Journal of the American Medical Association* 277: 32-37.

Krakow, B., P. L. Haynes, T. D. Warner, D. Melendrez, B. N. Sisley, L. Johnston, M. Hollifield, and S. Lee. 2007. Clinical sleep disorder profiles in a large sample of trauma survivors: An interdisciplinary view of posttraumatic sleep disturbance. *Sleep and Hypnosis* 9: 6-15.

Krakow, B., M. Hollifield, L. Johnston, M. Koss, R. Schrader, T. D. Warner, D. Tandberg, J. Lauriello, L. McBride, L. Cutchen, D. Cheng, S. Emmons, A, Germain, D. Melendrez, D. Sandoval, and H. Prince. 2001. Imagery rehearsal therapy for chronic nightmares in sexual assault survivors with posttraumatic stress disorder: A randomized controlled trial. *Journal of the American Medical Association* 286: 537-545.

Krakow, B. J., L. Johnston, D. Melendrez, M. Hollifield, T. D. Warner, D. Chavez-Kennedy, and M. J. Herlan. 2001. An open-label trial of evidence-based cognitive behavior therapy for nightmares and insomnia in crime victims with PTSD. *American Journal of Psychiatry* 158: 2043-2047.

Krakow, B. J., D. C. Melendrez, L. G. Johnston, J. O. Clark, E. M. Santana, T. D. Warner, M. A. Hollifield, R. Schrader, B. N. Sisley, and S. A. Lee. 2002. Sleep dynamic therapy for Cerro Grande fire evacuees with posttraumatic stress symptoms: A preliminary report. *Journal of Clinical Psychiatry* 63: 673-684.

Lamarche, L. J., and J. De Koninck. 2007. Sleep disturbance in adults with posttraumatic stress disorder: A review. *Journal of Clinical Psychiatry* 68: 1257-1270.

Mellman, T. A., V. Bustamente, A. I. Fins, W. R. Pigeon, and B. Nolan. 2002. REM sleep and the early development of posttraumatic stress disorder. *American Journal of Psychiatry* 159: 1696-1701.

Miller, W. R., and S. Rollnick. 2002. *Motivational Interviewing: Preparing People for Change.* 2nd ed. New York: Guilford Press.

Mohr, D., K. Vedantham, T. Neylan, T. J. Metzler, S. Best, and C. R. Marmar. 2003. The mediating effects of sleep in the relationship between traumatic stress and health symptoms in urban police officers. *Psychosomatic Medicine* 65: 485-489.

Morgan, K. 2000. Sleep and aging. In *Treatment of Late-Life Insomnia,* edited by K. L. Lichstein and C. M. Morin. Thousand Oaks, CA: Sage Publications.

Morin, C. M., C. Bastien, and J. Savard. 2003. Current status of cognitive-behavior therapy for insomnia: Evidence for treatment effectiveness and feasibility. In *Treating Sleep Disorders: Principles and Practice of Behavioral Sleep Medicine,* edited by M. Perlis and K. L. Lichstein. Hoboken, NJ : John Wiley & Sons.

Morin, C. M., and C. A. Espie. 2003. *Insomnia: A Clinical Guide to Assessment and Treatment.* New York: Kluwer Academic/Plenum Publishers.

Murray, B. 2002. Writing to heal. *Monitor on Psychology* 33: 54.

National Institutes of Health. Technology Assessment Panel. 1996. Integration of behavioral and relaxation approaches into the treatment of chronic pain and insomnia. *Journal of the American Medical Association* 276: 313-318.

Norris, F. H., and L. B. Slone. 2007. The epidemiology of trauma and PTSD. In *Handbook of PTSD: Science and Practice*, edited by M. J., Friedman, T. M. Keane, and P. A. Resick. New York: Guilford Press.

North, C. S., S. J. Nixon, S. Shariat, S. Mallonee, J. C. McMillen, E. L. Spitznagel, and E. M. Smith. 1999. Psychiatric disorders among survivors of the Oklahoma City bombing. *Journal of the American Medical Association* 282: 755-762.

Pennebaker, J. W. 1997. Writing about emotional experiences as a therapeutic process. *Psychological Science* 8: 162-166.

Pennebaker, J. W. 2004. *Writing to Heal: A Guided Journal for Recovering from Trauma and Emotional Upheaval.* Oakland, CA: New Harbinger Publications.

Pennebaker, J. W., J. Kiecolt-Glaser, and R. Glaser. 1988. Disclosure of traumas and immune function: Health implications for psychotherapy. *Journal of Consulting and Clinical Psychology* 56: 239-245.

Perlis, M. L., C. Jungquist, M. T. Smith, and D. Posner. 2008. *Cognitive and Behavioral Treatment of Insomnia: A Session-by-Session Guide.* New York: Springer.

Perlman, L. M., J. T. Arndt, L. Earnheart, A. A. Gorman, and K. G. Shirley. 2008. Group cognitive-behavioral therapy for insomnia in a VA mental health clinic. *Cognitive and Behavioral Practice* 15: 426-434.

Sandor, P., and C. M. Shapiro. 1994. Sleep patterns in depression and anxiety: Theory and pharmacological effects. *Journal of Psychosomatic Research* 38: 125-139.

Schell, T. L., G. N. Marshall, and L. H. Jaycox. 2004. All symptoms are not created equal: The prominent role of hyperarousal in the natural course of posttraumatic psychological distress. *Journal of Abnormal Psychology* 133: 179-197.

Smith, B., A. K. Ryan, D. L. Wingard, T. L. Patterson, D. J. Slymen, and C. A. Macera. 2008. Cigarette smoking and military deployment: A prospective evaluation. *American Journal of Preventive Medicine* 35: 539-546.

Smith, M., L. Smith, S. Nowakowski, and M. Perlis. 2003. Primary insomnia: Diagnostic issues, treatment, and future directions. In *Treating Sleep Disorders: Principles and Practice of Behavioral Sleep Medicine,* edited by M. Perlis and K. L. Lichstein. Hoboken, NJ: John Wiley & Sons.

Spielman, A. J., P. Saskin, and M. J. Thorpy. 1987. Treatment of chronic insomnia by restriction of time in bed. *Sleep* 10: 45-56.

Taylor, H. R., M. K. Feeman, and M. E. Cates. 2008. Prazosin for treatment of nightmares related to posttraumatic stress disorder. *American Journal of Health System Pharmacy* 65: 716-722.

Thompson, C. E., R. B. Taylor, M. E. McFall, R. F. Barnes, and M. A. Raskind. 2008. Nonnightmare distressed awakenings in veterans with posttraumatic stress disorder: Response to prazosin. *Journal of Traumatic Stress* 21: 417-420.

Wicklow, A., and C. A. Espie. 2000. Intrusive thoughts and their relationship to actigraphic measurement of sleep: Towards a cognitive model of insomnia. *Behaviour Research and Therapy* 38: 679-694.

Wohlgemuth, W. K., and J. D. Edinger. 2000. Sleep restriction therapy. In *Treatment of Late-Life Insomnia,* edited by K. L. Lichstein and C. M. Morin. Thousand Oaks, CA: Sage Publications.

World Health Organization. 1992. *The ICD-10 Classification of Mental and Behavior Disorders: Clinical Description and Diagnostic Guidelines.* Geneva: World Health Organization.

Karin Elorriaga Thompson, Ph.D., is clinical assistant professor at Tulane University School of Medicine, Department of Psychiatry and Behavioral Sciences, and a clinical psychologist at the VA Medical Center, Memphis, TN. She specializes in psychotherapy, clinical research, and assessment related to psychological trauma.

C. Laurel Franklin, Ph.D., is clinical assistant professor at Tulane University School of Medicine, Department of Psychiatry and Behavioral Sciences, and a clinical psychologist at the Southeast Louisiana Veterans Health Care System in New Orleans, LA. Her clinical and research interests are in the area of assessment and treatment of trauma-related problems, including post-traumatic stress disorder (PTSD).

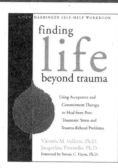
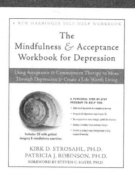